Jitsuo Morikawa

Biblical Dimensions of Church Growth

Judson Press ® Valley Forge

BIBLICAL DIMENSIONS OF CHURCH GROWTH

Library of Congress Cataloging in Publication Data

Morikawa, Jitsuo.
  Biblical dimensions of church growth.

  1. Church growth.   I. Title.
BV652.25.M67   262'.7   79-4040
ISBN 0-8170-0839-X

The name JUDSON PRESS is registered as a trademark in the U.S. Patent Office.
Printed in the U.S.A. ⊕

Introduction

Church growth has always been an issue of serious concern, but particularly so in recent years as signs of declining membership in main-line churches as well as in the Roman Catholic Church have been appearing. While the concept of growth has never been limited to numerical growth alone, this factor has played, without question, such a major role that while other factors and elements in the meaning of growth were recognized, numerical growth has been regarded the overriding symptom of vitality and the decline of membership the unquestioned sign of spiritual recession.

In the writer's judgment, the debate between quantity and quality, growth in size and growth in commitment, the relative merits of fast-growing denominations and those that are not, and the competitive evaluation of churches based on membership statistics appear to be futile. To assume that numerical largeness is a sign of neutralization of quality is as hazardous as to assume it is evidence of power. To presume that smallness is a result of high demand is equally as risky as to view recession as a sign of failure. Church growth is as complex and mysterious in its true nature as the growth of a life. There are no simple criteria for growth.

For this reason, a "Conference on Church Growth," sponsored by the Office of Evangelism of the American Baptist Churches' Board of National Ministries and held in Louisville, Kentucky, September 12-15, 1977, was most illuminating. Dr. Eric

Rust, of the Southern Baptist Theological Seminary, speaking as a scientist and theologian, was most provocative, especially in dealing with the unfinished and developmental nature of the universe and how church growth is a sign and witness to the growth of the universe toward completion. I am deeply indebted to him for presenting this vision of the gospel and underscoring insights from others, especially Dr. John B. Cobb, Jr., of the Claremont School of Theology.

Also during the conference, Dr. Orlando E. Costas, Director of the Latin American Evangelical Center for Pastoral Studies in San Jose, Costa Rica, with profound insight dealt with church growth as a multidimensional phenomenon. I am indebted to him specifically for the captions of numerical, reflective, organic, and transformative growth.

What I attempted to do was to forge into sermonic form what appear to me to be the various dimensions of church growth, relying on the cumulative insights drawn from many quarters, filtered through my own perceptions, and written in the immediacy of preaching each Sunday to a congregation of lay people. The material is not the product of studied research but the spontaneous dipping into the well of my own ruminations; it was written and delivered within the weekly demands of a parish congregation during an enjoyable interim ministry.

To reinforce lay awareness of the meaning, significance, and implications of church growth, this theme was pursued by the congregation as the subject for Lenten Bible studies, with close correlation between the preaching on Sunday mornings and the Bible study groups. (The Appendix describes more fully the way this process was developed in a local church.)

What became the exciting conviction to the writer was the overpowering reality of the growing universe, summoned by God "to grow up in every way into him who is the head, into Christ" (Ephesians 4:15). And the growth of the church is to be a sign and witness to the growth of the cosmos toward completion! We are indeed in a grand enterprise!

Contents

Chapters

Why Bible Study?

Christianity suffers more from its parody than from its substance, its caricature than from its reality, its distortions than from its true nature. No religious movement has been subject to such abuse and misunderstanding; and in the name of Christianity the most incredible, bizarre activities have been perpetrated, giving grounds for its discredit for those who have chosen their rejection. Enemies of the faith find ample forgeries and imitations of the faith, which perpetrate fraud and deceit on a credulous public.

But a far deeper problem Christianity suffers is the caricature of the faith which its most devoted members reject, and in rejecting the caricature, they reject the real substance. A whole lexicon of words has been outlawed from our world of religious respectability, and I mention only a few: evangelism, conversion, sin, everlasting life, and Bible study. The mention of these words conjures up images of the most bizarre behaviors and religious expressions which blind and constrain us. They seem to trigger for some the reliving and recollection of the most primitive religious expressions; and in the blinding light of that emotive reaction, these persons are unable to discern the true contours of meaning and significance. Therefore, we must consider and reconsider the place and power of Bible study as a central sacrament of the life of the church. Bible study is particularly important if we are to comprehend all the implications of "church growth"—a term too often used as a slogan.

I

It is one of the ironies of life that our childhood understanding of the Bible is regarded as normative throughout our lifetime. In no other realm of human experience would we consider our childhood perceptions as adequate. Our whole educational system, into the reaches and stretches of continuing education throughout one's adult years, enables us to keep abreast at least partially with the explosion of new knowledge, enabling us to deal with the increasing complexity of the modern world. The commonplace character of the Ph.D. degree—the rapidity with which its obsolescence occurs—is symbolic of the kind of world we live in; and yet, for some strange reason, even the very same persons caught up in the continuing pursuit of new knowledge possess an incredible naiveté when it comes to the knowledge of the Bible and the Christian faith and equate devotion to Jesus Christ with devotion to one's Sunday school perception and understanding of Jesus Christ. And to compound the perversity, there is often the assumption that the discarding of our childhood understanding of our faith is a mark of disloyalty and disaffection from the One who did say, "Except ye become as little children you cannot enter the kingdom." I doubt our Lord meant we retain a permanent childishness, but, rather, I think he meant to encourage in us a childlikeness, a trust, an insatiable curiosity, an eagerness to learn, an open mind, as well as a capacity for mirth and joy and incredible delight.

If we are attempting to imitate the early disciples—fishermen, unlettered and "untrained laymen"—the writings of Peter and John can hardly be classified as simple and childish. And despite our claim that the Bible was written in the "Koine" of common speech, presumably understood by peasant as well as priest, I see nothing approximating either the *Reader's Digest* or the *New York Daily News* in the style and substance of Paul's letter to the Romans.

We must overcome the typical American anti-intellectualism which dares to equate a life of faith with relaxation of our mental faculties and perversely to equate intellectual disciplines with a denial and dismissal of our faith in Jesus Christ. Jonathan Edwards is one of the few truly great thinkers and intellectual leaders in American history,[1] whose profound understanding of the gospel precipitated one of the great revival movements in our history. We have too long associated Christian faith's credibility and authenticity with simplicity bordering on ignorance, so that the same people who would sit through a symphony or an opera and take pride in their children's knowledge of calculus expect a sermon to be as simple as a story in a tabloid magazine. We are to love the Lord our God with all our heart and mind as well as all our soul and strength. Providing simple answers to complex problems in the field of medicine—and likewise in every sphere of life—is considered malpractice. Despite the appeal of oversimplification and the possibilities of wooing an adoring audience, we must deal honestly with reality. No easy answers are available; there are no shortcuts to eternal life, no six easy lessons into paradise. Such promises are to be distrusted. We must recommit ourselves to the arduous enterprise of thinking and living our life of faith; and to that end we must "keep alert with all perseverance" (Ephesians 6:18), in the words of Paul.

II

We happen to have been born into a world blessed with unprecedented, unrivaled biblical scholarship of the highest order. Our generation has been called one of the great moments in biblical and theological history, in which biblical scholarship matching the great days of Saint Augustine, Martin Luther, Thomas Aquinas, and John Calvin has emerged. Karl Barth and Rudolf Bultmann, the Niebuhrs and Tillich on the Protestant side of the aisle, and Karl Rahner and Hans Küng on the Catholic side are some of the luminous lights who have earned a place in the galaxy of shining lights. George Steiner of Cambridge and Geneva, not a theologian but a professor of English, in a recent *New York Times* editorial deplores the current decline in the arts and philosophy in Europe and America, but points to

> the striking renaissance of theological thought and argument. In terms of sheer force of insight, of adultness, of the gravity that honors the reader by taking his mental and moral capacities seriously, there is not much in recent philosophy or literature to match, let alone excel, the works of Rudolf Bultmann, of Karl Barth, of Karl Rahner, of Hans Küng (whose "To Be a Christian" is, just now, the most widely discussed book in Europe).
>
> Eberhard Bethge's biography of Dietrich Bonhoeffer is one of the few assured classics of our age, inexhaustible and uncompromising, as a classic must be. . . .[2]

Biblical scholarship must be pursued afresh in every new epoch in human history so that every new insight and every new knowledge in a world of growing knowledge might be recruited to bring new light and new illumination to our understanding of the Scriptures, which "bear witness to me," said Jesus (see John 5:39). Since the Bible points to and bears witness to ultimate reality, absolute reality, to Jesus Christ, every new insight of science, psychology, philosophy, arts, and history must be drafted as instruments to probe into the deeper meaning of the Scriptures. The Scriptures, on the other hand, must bring unfailing light in every epoch in human history; they must speak to the fundamental questions of the human race: "From whence have we come?" "Who are we?" and "Where are we going?" Without the light of the Bible we are a lost planet, groping in the darkness. What the psalmist long ago said is so true:

> Thy word is a lamp to my feet
> and a light to my path.
> —Psalm 119:105

That's why the great novelists of the ages, the great poets, great musicians, and great philosophers have relied heavily on biblical language, biblical imagery, and biblical truth as a way of probing reality to its subterranean depths.

That a small suppressed handful of people became a threat to history's greatest empire up to that moment and started a movement that shaped Western civilization for nineteen hundred years was due to the power of the Book which opened up a whole new horizon of hope for the human race and human civilization. Wherever this Book was read and studied, whether in secrecy or in public, churches were constituted, lives were born anew, human freedom and justice were demanded, slavery and tyranny were resisted, the universality of the human family was proclaimed, and parochialism was condemned.

We live in a society where the powerful impact of the Scriptures has so permeated our culture that we fail to distinguish between American culture and biblical culture; and seeing so many of the coinciding similarities between our American cultural aspirations and the biblical values, we have lost our sense of excitement and wonder of a new discovery of the Scriptures.

A little knowledge is often a dangerous thing when it impedes our pursuit of further knowledge; and the limited knowledge of the Scriptures as a prevailing condition of our culture has innoculated and immunized us from any pressing concern to study the Scriptures. The average person's capacity and willingness to expostulate on one's views of religion based on one's assumed knowledge of the Bible, some of which is ridiculously garbled and based on startling ignorance, is amazing. This is a strange state of affairs: politics and religion are two arenas of life in which everyone assumes intuitive expertise and claims legitimacy out of the assumption once voiced by President Eisenhower—that it doesn't matter what you believe, as long as you believe and have a faith. And many persons assume this is what the Bible teaches. Therefore, while the Bible still remains among the best sellers, the serious question is whether the Bible is actually being read and studied. The enormous publication of this Book of books is also contributing to our culture of extravagant waste, the waste not only of misuse but unuse, not only of being misread but unread. There is abundant biblical literature available, yet so many are illiterate; there are many libraries of study helps available but few who study the Book.

III

Why study the Bible? Because we cannot live without Christ, as Mother Teresa so movingly said, and we meet Christ and come to know him through his disclosures in the Scriptures. Both the Old Testament and the New testify to him; it is he to whom the prophets point; it is he who is the central actor in the drama of the Gospels; it is he about whom the exciting letters and epistles were written; so if we would meet him and be spoken to by him and be caught up by his power, we must meet him in the sacrament of the Word. Roman Catholics traditionally emphasized the sacrament of the Eucharist, the Protestants the sacrament of the Word, and both are essential.

Study of the Word places laypersons in equality before God. No priest, no preacher, no pastor need intervene between them and God. They are not dependent on the ministration of the sacrament by a priestly caste; every human soul, illumined by the Scriptures, is capable of being a priest to others. The reading and searching of the Scripture are open equally to all people. The sacrament of Bible study dramatizes the priesthood of all believers and the immediacy of the Christian's access to Christ through the open Book without either mediation or intervention of any priest or clergy.

Keys to the kingdom are not the sole possession of a particular clerical class. They dare not build their indispensability by such sacerdotal claims nor legitimate their role by any such claims of uniqueness. The Bible is an open book to which all have free access, which confirms the equality before God. All responsible Christians must affirm their priesthood by their access to the open Book.

The role of the preacher and pastor is to heighten and quicken the laity's desire to search the Scriptures. We of the clergy are not employed to study the Bible for you, to meet Christ on your behalf, to be a proxy for you so that you live with compensatory delight in your pastor's biblical and theological knowledge, while you remain untroubled with your ignorance. His or her biblical acquaintance is no substitute for your acquaintance. His or her theological enterprise cannot possibly take the place of your theological enterprise. His or her role and responsibility is to enable the whole congregation to become astute students of the Bible, to enable the whole congregation to become lay theologians.

Let me remind you that John Calvin was a layman, a lawyer who regarded the study of the Scriptures as essential and imperative, and his diligent studies are reflected in his famous *Institutes of the Christian Religion*. Hendrick Kraemer, the great Dutch theologian, was a layman. Jacques Ellul, whose theological writings are voraciously read, is a layman, a professor of law in a French university. If it's important to master a particular discipline in our culture—be it economics, medicine, law, education, or any of the physical and social sciences—it is equally important to wrestle with the ultimate framework and the final context of every discipline and human enterprise; and this is precisely what biblical and theological studies are about. They deal with the total landscape of history—its beginning and end, history and beyond history, what is visible and invisible, what is contemporary and transcendent—with life and death, with time and eternity, with collapse and resurrection, with finiteness and infinity, with the temporal and immortal.

What a grand enterprise is the theological enterprise! What exciting horizons of hope are available to those who study the Scriptures!

> Blessed is the man
> who walks not in the counsel of the wicked,
> nor stands in the way of sinners,
>   nor sits in the seat of scoffers;
> but his delight is in the law of the LORD,

and on his law he meditates day and night.
He is like a tree
    planted by streams of water,
that yields its fruit in its season,
    and its leaf does not wither.
In all that he does, he prospers

—Psalm 1:1-3

2 Are
We Growing?

"My, you have grown!" is an expression we heard over and over again in our childhood; it almost bordered on a form of salutation. It is an expression of delight and surprise, adding to the festal atmosphere of family and social life. In recent weeks I have seen the miracle of growth in a little baby. Each week the marks of growth are so visibly evident: a new face, a new size since she is so quickly outgrowing her little garments, eyes which seem to see, and new strength in her arms and legs. Gradually the likeness of her father's image has emerged, but then in a few weeks she may reappear with a semblance of her mother's beautiful face. Also, in one of our home meetings, I had the delight of seeing two persons I had known as adolescents some fifteen years ago, but now they are grown into manhood and womanhood. The awkward signs of adolescence are fully shed, and now they exhibit all the polished marks of adulthood.

Growth is a fundamental character of life, a sign of life—the central sign of life, so that life and growth are synonymous and the cessation of growth akin to death—and this is also true in the life of the church. Are we able to greet our congregation and say with salutary zest: "My, but it has grown; there is such a difference today from what it was—a new spirit, a new air, a new, indescribable something!" Can we say that? Are we outgrowing our conceptual garments and theological cribs so that we need larger concepts and sturdier intellectual underpinnings? Are we shedding some of our adolescent verve and taking on a more cool and collected character of adults? Are we troubled that we have ceased growing physically? We had hoped to achieve the American model of 6' 4", but it seems we have to settle for less. Is the question of church growth a serious question, a way of testing out who we are, gauging and evaluating our health, a way of measuring our stature, examining our identity?

Does the concept of growth provide the indexes by which we measure our obedience and loyalty to Jesus Christ, so that we may determine whether we are growing "in wisdom and in stature, and in favor with God and man" (Luke 2:52), whether there is an imbalance in our growth or a proper symmetry in our development, a gracefulness of proportion and balanced equilibrium in our body?

This book will pursue the theme of "church growth." We invite you to participate in critical Bible study classes, to examine the health and constitution of your church, therefore your health and constitution, measured against biblical norms. Let me give you a little taste of what to expect when we search the Scriptures related to the question "Are we growing?"

I

The Bible's view of the cosmos is that we are living in an unfinished, developmental universe, a growing universe, a changing universe, and that the purpose of God is for the whole universe "to grow up in every way into him who is the head, into Christ" (Ephesians 4:15). The fundamental purpose of God for this world is growth and development. A world which began in "the garden" (see Genesis 2:15) will finally end in a city, "the holy city, new Jerusalem, coming down out of heaven" (Revelation 21:2), which means at least that what began in primitive simplicity and virgin wilderness will end in urban complexity that in the face of density has mastered the art of community, miniaturizing the mechanisms of human industry, according to Paolo Soleri, to survive in a world of shrinking space. What began with open spaces and life freed and nurtured by distance and the propulsive pull of infinity will end with the impulsive power of proximity, in which nearness and closeness of crowded cities and urban communities will create new living tissues of human discourse and interdependence.

The Bible's view of the growth of faith is spectacular and awe inspiring. Abraham stands out in the vast history of the human race as the architect of a life of faith, a life lived in obedience to God—obedience to God which is prior to obedience to family or nation. And what a vision of growth and development is anticipated: "And I will make of you a great nation, and I will bless you, and make your name great, so that you will be a blessing.... And by you all the families of the earth shall bless themselves" (Genesis 12:2-3)—the growth from one to the "all"! What began with one solitary man of faith in the remote horizon of the past will end with descendants "as many as the stars of heaven and as the innumerable grains of sand by the seashore" (Hebrews 11:12). One person lit a light of faith and hope in a world of darkness, pointing toward the day in the distant future when candles of faith and love will be lit in every home in every nation under the sun, and the "sun of righteousness shall rise, with healing in its wings" (Malachi 4:2). The entire world will be populated by heirs of Abraham, people of faith, who will live lives of obedience to God, who will "obey God rather than men" (Acts 5:29).

The Bible's view of growth from anarchy to order is also impressive. The whole cosmic story begins with chaos. "In the beginning of creation, when God made heaven and earth, the earth was without form and void, with darkness over the face of the abyss, and a mighty wind that swept over the surface of the waters" (Genesis 1:1-2, NEB). But chaos grows and emerges into order: "God said, 'Let there be light,' and there was light" (Genesis 1:3). And this order of creation from primeval abyss to the creation of heaven and earth, from chaos to cosmos, is not only primordial history but is also the biblical vision of the total drama of history, a world in moral disarray through the subversive presence of human sin, changing and growing up "in every way into him who is the head, into Christ" (Ephesians 4:15). What a contrast! What prospects of change and development and growth! A world in confusion and chaos eventually becoming an embodiment of Jesus Christ, incarnating the presence of God in human history (Romans 11:36; Ephesians 1:22)!

II

But the Bible's view of the whole cosmos "to grow up in every way into him who is the head, into Christ" seems incredibly contradictory, to say the least. It sounds like a process of compression, of squeezing the breadth of the universe into the confining contours of the life of Christ—a seemingly impossible metaphor and figure of speech. This perplexity arises out of the assumption that Christ is also a product of earth, that the world preceded him, that he also is an event in history, one among many even if he is first among them all. That is the reason why we raise the questions "How can we claim his finality and ultimacy in the presence of many others that are claimed to be saviors of earth?" and "How do we resolve the particularity of Christ and the Bible's claim to his universality?"

Christ is not a creature of earth: "In him all things were created, in heaven and on earth . . . all things were created through him and for him. He is before all things, and in him all things hold together" (Colossians 1:16-17). Jesus Christ is from everlasting to everlasting; the cosmos has a beginning and an end, a moment of conception and a time of consummation, and it is the object of the creative activity of Jesus Christ—he is subject; he is Creator; he initiates, brings into existence "out of nothing"; and what he began he will complete. Since creation is the product of his power, an extension of his being, then marks of his presence are everywhere: "The heavens are telling the glory of God . . ." (Psalm 19:1); "and the kingdom of God is at hand" (Mark 1:15). Jesus Christ is not only in the world, but also the world is in Jesus Christ—embraced by him, loved by him, sustained by him, held together by him, therefore subject to him, even as the body is subject to the head, as creature to creator, as object to subject, as finite to infinite.

This is what is meant when we read "For as in Adam all die, so also in Christ shall all be made alive" (1 Corinthians 15:22). In the crucifixion and death of one Jesus Christ, the crucifixion and death of the whole world occurred; therefore we all can say, "I am crucified with Christ . . ." (Galatians 2:20), dead and buried. We can also say: "For if we have been united with him in a death like his, we shall certainly be united with him in a resurrection like his" (Romans 6:5). The death of Jesus Christ is universal; it represents the death of the whole world which is in Christ. And his life and resurrection are also universal; it represents the resurrection of the whole cosmos embraced in Christ. Therefore, the death and resurrection of Christ are not simply personal events but cosmic events of universal scope, events of order out of chaos, formlessness which is without aim and goal taking the shape of purpose and future, the cosmic void and abyss being filled with the quickening presence of God. The Bible's three major themes are creation, redemption, and consummation. They are all universal in scope, and they are all christological in origin: in Christ the world came into being (Colossians 1:16); in Christ shall all be made alive (1 Corinthians 15:22); and finally Christ shall "unite all things in him" (Ephesians 1:10). We have come to know Jesus Christ as personal Savior and Lord, but that is a very limited view of him. We must also know him as Creator of the cosmos, Shaper of history, cosmic Redeemer, universal Sovereign, the overarching will and mind, the "ground of being," the universal Spirit, the soul of the cosmos. "He's got the world in his hands; he's got the whole world in his hands."

Therefore, we have the Bible's view of the whole cosmos: "to grow up in every way into him who is the head, into Christ" (Ephesians 4:15). As a little babe grows, it takes on the likeness of the ones from whom it was conceived. The whole universe is growing into the likeness of the One through whom conception, creation, redemption, and consummation occur.

III

In the meantime, at this time in God's history, while the church has been waiting for the whole cosmos "to grow up in every way into him," it has emerged as little islands of anticipation, harbingers of cosmic hope, firstfruits of harvest. The church is the first sign of the coming of springtime; it is made up of little colonies anticipating God's commonwealth. So the questions of the church must be: Are we growing in such a way that we become signs of the growth of the cosmos into the image of Christ? Is this little piece of the cosmos, our church, an image of Christ, the body of Christ, in Christ, crucified with him, and raised with him, living in the power of Christ's resurrection, shedding the "old creature," "the old man," "the persons we once were"?

Are we a people of the future or a people of a past? Are we desperately holding on to a past which is passing away, or are we hopefully facing the future for new possibilities to emerge? Do you mean to tell me that the days of heroism and the call to courage and the opening of new horizons are all in the past, that there are no real issues to confront, no tyrannies to battle, no new dimensions of life to explore? Do you mean to tell me that there is no one in the immediate horizon with the charisma and courage of leadership to equal those in the past? Or is the future shaping and raising up a new tribe of leadership, a new creative ministry, a new form of integrity and courage? Newness is in the air; we cannot survive on yesterday's achievements, anymore than Israel could be nurtured on yesterday's manna (Exodus 16:19). "Morning by morning they gathered it . . ." (Exodus 16:21). Every new day is a new beginning, the laying claim to a new future, having access to a heretofore unknown world, a new age, new dimensions of "the breadth and length and height and depth" (Ephesians 3:18) ". . . [of] the hope to which he has called you, . . . [of] the riches of his glorious inheritance . . . , [of] the immeasurable greatness of his power . . ." (Ephesians 1:18-19).

Remember the days during the fifties and sixties when the church-school enrollment taxed buildings and we had to build educational annexes? They were the great days of Christian education, we say. Does that mean that in the economy of God growth and development peaked in those years and now we are in an era of decline and contraction? Whatever form it takes, growth into newness means shedding the marks of every lively temporality—whether infancy, childhood, adolescence, with all their growing dynamism—and taking on new forms and signs of growth and development. Churches must enter a new stage and level of growth, and they will in all probability take on new forms and new styles and new structures as compared to their exciting past. The whole world is moving so fast into the future, swiftly toward God's goal and purpose of completion and maturity, "to grow up in every way" (Ephesians 4:15), that we cannot afford to be living in the past and be left behind, anachronic, outdated, and out of step. We must always be "running" (see Hebrews 12:1) and pressing on toward the future, tackling the battlements and ramparts which seek to keep us out of the future, assaulting and laying siege to all the magnificent fortifications built by contemporary civilization to confine us as prisoners of the present and past.

James Reston, America's leading journalist pulpiteer, points us to Lincoln and his growth into the presidency. He writes,

In his "Calendar of Great Americans," Woodrow Wilson made an observation about Mr. Lincoln which still stands as a fairly good test of American Presidents at the end of their first year in the White House.

"The most significant thing about the career of the man [Lincoln]," Wilson wrote, "is the way in which he grew steadily into a national stature . . . [and] as he grew, everything formed, informed, transformed him. The process was slow but unbroken. He was not fit to be President until he actually became President. He was fit then, because learning everything as he went, he had found out how much there was to learn. . . ."[1]

Are we growing steadily into churchly stature, learning everything as we go, and finding out how much there is to learn? We are "to grow up in every way into him, who is the head, into Christ" (Ephesians 4:15).

3
Unfinished Creation

A static view of the universe prevails: a world created in the infinite past in all its natural grandeur, eroding and wasting away by constant use and perennial abuse. We tend to compare it to all human creations, vaunted civilizations and cultures which grow old in time and gradually disappear. This sense of earth's finiteness has been dramatically felt and faced because of the threat of exhaustion of the world's oil resources and the imminent disappearance of the great monster of the sea, the whale. Men and women, called by God to be partners in the shaping of the global enterprise, have abused that privilege, betrayed that trust, even as officers of the Teamsters Union were charged with failure "to carry out their fiduciary responsibilities to manage the [pension] fund's assets prudently."[1] The earth and its prudent management have been placed in our trust by God; we are the trustees of this global endowment. But negligence has been our history, carelessness the style of our stewardship; we have been lax in observance of laws and regulations to protect our environment. Fraudulent behavior so current in business and government is a reflection of the ways in which we have over the centuries defrauded the earth.

I

But we cannot lose sight that we live in an unfinished, developmental universe, a growing universe, caught in the ten-

23

sion of "contingency and order," "chaos always standing on the boundary of order, threatening to invade it and destroy its structures," in the words of Eric Rust.[2] On the other hand, Rust goes on to say: "God created the world with a potential for perfection, with all the potencies and powers that would make its ultimate perfection possible. He created it so that His purpose might ultimately be fulfilled. . . ."[3]

We are obsessed with the sense of age—the age of rocks, the age of the planet, the age of the universe—and we equate age with decline and deterioration. There is an assumption that this earth and world had an early stage of grandeur and beauty in its unmolested youth, a pristine beauty unspoiled, untouched, and uncorrupted by human commerce; but after these billions of years of natural history and millions of years of human history, our universe is in a stage of old age, with the ravages of time apparent in its countenance, showing signs of exhaustion rather than replenishment, of decline more than growth, of wasted years rather than future hope. Our frenzied search for youth, the cult of the young, the desperate effort to prolong our youthful years with every cosmetic collaboration, is a loud indicator that we think we are part of a spent and static universe.

What a tragic view we have, as though the planets were hurled into space and left, winding down or wearing out to a final point of extinction! Rather, we live in a universe that is in constant process of renewal and growth. The Bible speaks of this encompassing cosmic renewal in personal terms, reduced and miniaturized into manageable terms: "If any one is in Christ, he is a new creation; the old has passed away, behold, the new has come" (2 Corinthians 5:17). The new has come; the new age, the new humanity, the new man, and the new woman have come, confronting the old, challenging death and dying, battling and waging war against intimidating threats against the aging. This means that every new day is a new beginning unlike any days of the past, providing new frontiers of reality, a new world, new perceptions, new meaning, and new significance. "[The Lord's true love and compassion] are new every morning; so great is his constancy" (Lamentations 3:23, NEB). And the older we grow in our years, the closer we come to the new, because the whole cosmos is growing, replacing the old barks and the superfluous with new growth of new tissues, until the cosmos becomes finally, totally new, "a new heaven and a new earth" (Revelation 21:1). "The universe itself is to be freed from the shackles of mortality and enter upon the liberty and splendour of the children of God. Up to the present, we know, the whole created universe groans in all its parts as if in the pangs of childbirth" (Romans 8:21-22, NEB).

The world and the cosmos as it grows older in its years becomes newer, in prospect, full of novelty, disclosing surprises out of the subterranean depths of its being and soul. This cosmic vision is again personalized by the Hebrew psalmist:

> The righteous flourish like a palm-tree,
> they grow tall as a cedar on Lebanon;
>> planted as they are in the house of the LORD,
>> they flourish in the courts of our God,
> vigorous in old age like trees full of sap,
>> luxuriant, wide-spreading,
> eager to declare that the Lord is just,
> The LORD my rock, in whom there is no unrighteousness.
>> —Psalm 92:12-15(NEB)

"Flourish like a palm-tree!" "Grow tall as a cedar on Lebanon!" Be "vigorous in old age like trees full of sap, luxuriant, wide-spreading, eager to declare that the Lord is just." The God in whom you trust and declare is just is One who says, "Behold! I am making all things new!" (Revelation 21:5, NEB);

> Behold, I am doing a new thing;
>> now it springs forth, do you not perceive it?
> I will make a way in the wilderness,
>> rivers in the desert.
>> —Isaiah 43:19

"I will give them a different heart and put a new spirit into them" (Ezekiel 11:19, NEB). The whole ministry of Jesus Christ is the inauguration of the new: through the blood of the new covenant, through giving us a new commandment, he encourages us to drink of the new wine to celebrate the new age, in which "out of the two [i.e., Jews and Gentiles] a single new humanity" (Ephesians 2:15, NEB) is created.

II

But the growth toward completion and maturity of our unfinished developmental universe is not a gradual, persistent, inevitable growth, as though an internal principle in the universe was asserting its predetermined intention and course. Eric Rust writes: Even "modern science is making us increasingly aware of the chaotic, contingent, random aspects of our world. The desert always lies on the edge of the garden."[4] There is nothing unerring and relentless about our universe; it is not a glacial wilderness of impersonality, bound to the mechanisms of natural forces and physical laws, but a sacramental universe with a living soul.

We must be reminded again and again that the doctrine of incarnation means not only "the Word became flesh" (John 1:14), God in the world, but also the world in God, so that, in the words of Dietrich Bonhoeffer, "in Christ the reality of God entered into the reality of the world,"[5] and in Christ the reality of God and the reality of the world are united.[6] Stated in the language of Paul, the whole cosmos is "to grow up in every way into him who is the head, into Christ" (Ephesians 4:15) so that even as the church is the body of Christ, ultimately the whole universe will "body forth" Jesus Christ, when "Christ is all, and in all" (Colossians 3:11); "for from him and through him and to him are all things" (Romans 11:36). This means that we are part of a spiritual universe, not a mechanistic world operated by impersonal laws, but a universe presided over by a living Lord, whom God has raised "above all rule and authority and power and dominion, and above every name that is named . . . and he has put all things under his feet and has made him the head over all things . . ." (Ephesians 1:21-22). We as cosmos and world are united with Christ our head, and "in him we live and move and have our being" (Acts 17:28); we are divinely interrelated, as body to head, branches to vine. We are in Christ even as Christ is in us, but the will and purpose of Christ the head is never exercised in lonely isolation or ignoring independence of the body; rather, it is exercised in loving fellowship and communion and communication with his body.

He does not merely pronounce his will and edict and declare his unalterable purpose, but he entreats and beseeches and implores and begs and woos for our love and obedience like Hosea, the prophet who with entreating compassion went in search of his unfaithful wife to win her back (Hosea 3:1). By incarnating himself in the hungry, the thirsty, the stranger, the naked, and the sick and pleading for our love through the outstretched hands of the weak (Matthew 25:35-36), and even by his relentless, unerring judgment on all sin and his conviction and condemnation on every fraudulent behavior, Christ seeks to win us. But "he himself bore our sins in his body on the tree" (1 Peter 2:24); "he was wounded for our transgressions, he was bruised for our iniquities" (Isaiah 53:5).

Therefore, the growth toward maturity of our unfinished universe is not a natural growth, like the growth of a tree, but the growth of a divine-human community, full of contingency and order, chaos and unity, sin and renewal, regression and growth, death and resurrection. No romantic optimism rooted in the belief of evolutionary growth toward maturity and completion is a credible posture to assume in this highly moral universe. Nor is the opposite alternative to a static universe, winding down by erosion and wear to an eventual point of extinction and death, a credible posture. We are part of a moral universe, of which Jesus Christ is head and we are the body, a universe engaged in the strife and struggle of the cosmos growing up "in every way into Christ," growing out of the "swaddling clothes" of infancy into the unsymmetry of adolescence, and finally into the wholeness of maturity. And this growth occurs through call and obedience, through lordship and loyalty, through God's gift and human thanksgiving. The growth of the universe into newness occurs at the conjunction of the freedom of God and the freedom of humanity exercising their freedom of choice in a collaborative enterprise, involved in the tension and agony and pain of the moral struggle toward life.

Just as our lives bear the scars of conflict and pain, these dwarfed areas of our being which fear and unbelief have kept in intimidating repression, so the universe tragically shows great areas of underdevelopment. Need our notion of the underdeveloped nations and areas of our world be equated with the so-called Third World? Aren't there huge gaps of underdevelopment in the Western nations, in Europe and America also? When we ignore these underdeveloped areas in the Western world, aren't we exhibiting a one-dimensional perception of reality?[7] Our "practical atheism"?[8] Our anti-Marxist ideology contradicted by our materialistic life-style? Our absence of an eschatology in the face of a Marxist eschatology? Our indulgent style of life in a world of revolutionary asceticism of the Chinese?

III

What is the relation between the unfinished character of the universe and church growth? Church growth must be a continuous sign and witness in this world that we are, in fact, in a universe which is constantly confronting the emergence of newness. How? The church must demonstrate in its life and fellowship that new frontiers of human social hope are actually being pressed and realized, that "the new being"[9] is being experienced, that "the new creation" is becoming visible, that some signs of "the new age" are present.

For one thing, a church becomes a sign of a growing universe by seeing hope and possibility in every life; by seeing that no life is hopeless, beyond redemption, that no life is wasted beyond recovery, no person misshapen beyond corrective surgery, no person so desperate as to be without hope. We live in a world which is morally indifferent yet cruelly calculating, a world bound to the dispassionate assumption of the unerring operation of the law of cause and effect, so that every tragic consequence is accepted as a result of some antecedent misdemeanor. Each life is left on his or her own to work out his or her own destiny, and if he or she fails and collapses, it's too bad; if he or she succeeds, he or she really made it. Such impersonality and such indifference! To think we live in a universe where, whether we live or whether we die, no one really cares. As long as we serve a useful purpose, we are remembered; when we are no longer useful, we are nonexistent. This attitude is a sign of the old creation, the old state of things, the law operating in the old age, which is passing away (see 2 Corinthians 5:17). But in the new age, in the new creation begun in Jesus Christ, human life and destiny are determined and shaped by grace and mercy. Hope and forgiveness, renewal and salvation are extended to everyone. No one is irretrievably beyond the scope of redemption. The church is the place in the world where the hopeless find hope, the wasted find recovery, the new creation begins to triumph over the old.

The church's radical new perception toward the aging and the old in our society becomes a sign of a universe growing toward the emergence of newness. We live in a society succumbed to the cruel myth of "aging as a way to the darkness," write Walter Gaffney and Henri Nouwen,[10] when in actuality the new age in Jesus Christ has made possible "aging as a way to the light."[11] Recall Simeon in his old age coming into the temple and seeing the child Jesus, taking him up in his arms and saying,

> "Lord, now lettest thou thy servant depart in peace . . .
>   for mine eyes have seen thy salvation."
>   —Luke 2:29-30

Remember Moses telling his people: "Ask . . . [of] your elders, and they will tell you" (Deuteronomy 32:7). Gaffney and Nouwen write:

The darkness of old age has been pretty well documented, but the light does not seem to fit into the computers and tabulation machines of the profit-makers. However, concerned people today are beginning to dispel the mythological aspects of growing old. They are convinced that much of the fear of becoming old in young and middle-aged people is based more on rumors than on facts.[12]

They go on to say:

We think of old Pope John giving life to an old church, and of old Mother Teresa offering hope to the sick and dying in India. We look at the last self-portrait of Rembrandt and discover a depth that was not there before. We marvel at the last works of Michelangelo and realize they are his best. We remember the strong face of the old Schweitzer, the piercing eyes of the elderly Einstein, and the mild face of Pope Pius X.[13]

We are not living in a universe in its old age winding down to erosion and extinction; we are living in a growing universe, leaving in its wake the scattered remnants of decay and death, but ever in ceaseless pursuit of horizons of newness. As an essential part of that growing universe, the church must grow out of its old mortifying myths of old age and grow up "having the eyes of [its] heart enlightened, that [it] may know" (Ephesians 1:18) that old age is actually flirtation on the boundaries of consummation, exploring the depth and the height of the love of God, having traversed its breadth and length (see Ephesians 3:18). "For salvation is nearer to us now than when we first believed; the night is far gone, the day is at hand" (Romans 13:11-12).

4 The Ultimate End of Church Growth

We are living in a society that is terribly confused and reluctant to know the purpose of our human enterprise. What is the purpose of business and industry? Beyond the crass motive of profit as the bottom line, the whole mechanism of the industrial enterprise propels on motivation which is short sighted and uninspiring. Kenneth Boulding, the economist, "rejects the doctrine, traditional in his profession, that economics is, and ought to be, concerned only with means and not ends,"[1] but his is a rare voice crying in the wilderness. No wonder our economy suffers such cycles of boom and recession. And giant corporations, which ideologically believe in free enterprise, resist government intervention when they are robust and flowering, but they plead for government intervention in the marketplace when they are unable to compete with foreign counterparts.

For years, the university has been struggling to know its purpose; this struggle is dramatically laid out by President Clark Kerr in his book *The Uses of the University*.

The appointment of a new president at Yale has again surfaced the issue. In response to questions addressed to President A. Bartlett Giamatti, he spoke of the formlessness of the curriculum at Yale, by which he meant the absence of "an informing principle for the growth of the curriculum. . . . It's precisely because of the complexity of knowledge," he said, "that

31

we have to go back and find out what our Judeo-Christian culture consists of. . . . That's our heritage."[2]

What is true in the world of business and education is pervasively true in our culture: we don't know why and to what end we are engaged in our human enterprise beyond the most obvious and immediate concerns of survival, personal welfare, self-interest, and achievement of success; and when these are realized, we are left in basic discontent, and every goal fulfilled appears somewhat hollow and meaningless. Why? Because our culture is not informed by an eschatology.

I

The instant reaction to the term "eschatology" proves a point. Most of us don't even know what it means, and those who claim some knowledge associate it with death and the end. But to most the term is irrelevant, another piece of theological jargon having little relationship to reality, especially to daily practical living. Unfortunately language is one of the clearest indicators of our beliefs and values, even as art and drama are revealers and disclosers of our collective soul. When our daily language—in conversation, in our news, and in our shoptalk of the marketplace—never touches on eschatology, it means we have no eschatology; we are so bankrupt that we even stoop to its derision. We smile with a sense of amusement and worldly wisdom that one could be so anachronistic, out of date, passé, as to take seriously such an unreal and remote notion when the central business of life has to do with technology and production and economic growth, not eschatology. Economic growth seems to be the dominant preoccupation of our nation today, whether it's Henry Ford's charge that "the country's economy had been 'trussed-up' and seriously impeded by a 'growing web' of Federal rules and interference,"[3] or Vernon Jordan's call for full employment by government and private sectors in collaborative teamwork.

There is no question that we cannot live without bread and that the fact of millions of unemployed is a scandal of our civilization, especially in an affluent nation like the U.S.A. But the nation's engrossed preoccupation with economic growth, abstracted and isolated from the larger context of eschatology, suggests that we believe we shall live by bread alone. But "man shall not live by bread alone, but by every word that proceeds from the mouth of God" (Matthew 4:4).

This preoccupation with economic growth is actually

evidence of what a low view of life we have. We assume we are basically physical beings, part of the animal kingdom, possessed with the instinct of survival, with needs of hunger and sex and fellowship to satisfy, living out threescore and ten years and then quietly vanishing from the earth. To make our way in the world in as dignified a way as possible is the normative ambition of most people. Most of us operate within the small parameter of our family, of our children; and any sense of future we have is only in terms of their welfare. Our view of reality is so small, our vision so limited that we are slowly perishing of suffocation from the smallness of our universe. We long for space, but we live in the crowded corridors of our little circumscribed world. We are made for eternity, but we compress ourselves into time. We are lured by vision, but we deny ourselves vision in order to settle for immediate satisfaction and instant answers to our problems.

II

We need an eschatology, "the doctrine of the last things," a view of the final end toward which this universe is moving and rushing; we need a view which does not see this end as a terminal point, extinction, or death and final dissolution, but consummation and completion. We can compare the universe to little streams originating out of the hills and mountains and forests, emptying into the river, which in turn winds its way through treacherous rapids and narrow gorges, across the plains, past villages and towns and great cities, ever widening its banks and deepening its channels, until finally it empties into the open sea to become swallowed by oceanic depths.

We read in the Scriptures: "For he has made known to us in all wisdom and insight the mystery of his will, according to his purpose which he set forth in Christ as a plan for the fulness of time, to unite all things in him, things in heaven and things on earth" (Ephesians 1:9-10). The great gap and distance between heaven and earth, dream and reality, vision and realization, hope and fulfillment will be overcome. The yawning chasms of a divided world will be completely filled, the iron curtains of hostile nations dismantled:

"and they shall beat their swords into plowshares
    and their spears into pruning hooks."
    —Isaiah 2:4

The wolf shall dwell with the lamb,

and the leopard shall lie down with the kid,
and the calf and the lion and the fatling together,
and a little child shall lead them.
—Isaiah 11:6

Again we read in the Scriptures: "For in him all the fulness of God was pleased to dwell, and through him to reconcile to himself all things, whether on earth or in heaven, making peace by the blood of his cross" (Colossians 1:19-20). "To reconcile to himself all things"—what a hopeful vision! God's ultimate purpose will not be frustrated. He will not finally bring creation to an end, rescuing a little handful in a Noah's ark, or saving a tiny remnant while the vast majority of humanity ends in destruction. The biblical vision and the great heart of God do not thrive on exclusivism and rejection but embrace inclusion, "not willing that any should perish, but that all should come to repentance" (2 Peter 3:9, KJV). God does not stoop to the appeal of elitism, nor does he sympathize with our moral insistence on the damnation of others. Outside of Christ there is no life, "for there is no other name under heaven given among men by which we must be saved" (Acts 4:12). And Jesus said with finality: "I am the way, and the truth, and the life; no one comes to the Father, but by me" (John 14:6). This does not mean that outside the church there is no salvation. But outside of Christ there is no salvation. The good news of the gospel, according to Colossians, is: "For in him all the fulness of God was pleased to dwell, and through him to reconcile to himself all things, whether on earth or in heaven . . ." (Colossians 1:19-20). The breadth and depth and height of God's love and mercy are reflected in the recurrence of the Greek word *panta*, meaning "all things." "All things were created through him"; "He is before all things"; "in him all things hold together"; "He reconciles to himself all things"; all things, all things, all things!

In fact "God has highly exalted him [Christ] and bestowed on him the name which is above every name, that at the name of Jesus every knee should bow, in heaven and on earth and under the earth, and every tongue confess that Jesus Christ is Lord, to the glory of God the Father" (Philippians 2:9-11). At the completion and consummation of God's purpose for the universe, "every knee should bow" and "every tongue confess that Jesus Christ is Lord."

III

The power of eschatology, the doctrine of Christian hope,

resides not only in "the object hoped for," as we have delineated, but also in "the hope inspired by it," in the words of Jürgen Moltmann. "From first to last, and not merely in the epilogue, Christianity is eschatology, is hope, forward looking and forward moving, and therefore also revolutionizing and transforming the present."[4]

The exciting thing about Christian eschatology is that it does not push the "end" and "last things" to an infinite future, but asserts that the "end" has already begun; the final future of God is already confronting the present; "the end" is not only in sight, but also we are already parties and participants in it. In Hebrews we read: "When in former times God spoke to our forefathers, he spoke in fragmentary and varied fashion through the prophets. But in this the final age he has spoken to us in the Son" (Hebrews 1:1-2, NEB), as "the *complete* 'last' dealings of God with humanity," in the words of Hans J. Margull.[5] The whole Gospel of John is eschatological; it claims the future now; the final age is in the present, so that everlasting life is a present possession; we drink of the living water now (John 4:13-14) and eat of the living bread and shall not hunger (John 6:35). When John the Baptist was in prison perplexed, he sent messengers to Jesus to ask: "Are you he who is to come, or shall we look for another?" (Matthew 11:2-3). Are you the Messiah, or do we still wait for him? And Jesus answered them, "Go and tell John what you hear and see: the blind receive their sight and the lame walk, lepers are cleansed and the deaf hear, and the dead are raised up, and the poor have good news preached to them" (Matthew 11:4-5). These are all signs of the Messianic Age, that the "end" has come, "the final age" has begun, the final future of God is inaugurated. "Behold, the kingdom of God is in the midst of you" (Luke 17:21). Jesus cast out demons, a consummate sign: "But if it is by the finger of God that I cast out demons," said Jesus, "then the kingdom of God has come upon you" (Luke 11:20).

The transformative power of eschatology resides in the fact that the ultimate goal and end of history, God's purpose for the universe, is what Christianity is all about. To be sure, within that cosmic comprehension, the salvation of every human life is essential. But the central focus of the Bible is not the salvation and destiny of each individual person, but the renewal and growth and transformation of the whole cosmos into the new heaven and the new earth (Revelation 21:1). Therefore "church growth" must be clearly understood in the light of the ultimate end. Is the growth of the church affecting and witnessing to the fact that we are in the "final age," the "last days," living in "the power of an endless life" (Hebrews 7:16), that we are actually a messianic people feasting at the messianic table, already enjoying eternal life and living in the power of the Spirit promised for the last days and poured out on all flesh so that "your sons and your daughters shall prophesy, and your young men shall see visions, and your old men shall dream dreams" (Acts 2:17)?

Is our church growing in perception and size and compassion, enabling it in God's grace to embrace the whole world, to love all and to affirm all humankind and the whole universe? Have we outgrown our adolescent prejudices of nationalism, racial arrogance, and class pride to become universally identified with the whole world and the whole cosmos? That is the "impossible possibility" to which we are called. Have we outgrown our self-absorbed concern only for our own salvation and focused on the salvation of the whole world, that is, to "unite all things in him," overcoming every dividing alienation and separation, be it economic, political, moral, social, or spiritual?

The unity of the whole world in Christ is the vision and activity to which the church must grow. We have a larger task than that of wrestling with the unity and oneness of one little congregation, with our little differences and divisions and sometimes alienations. The unity of the whole world, the reconciliation of the cosmos, is our agenda! This task is largely beyond us—beyond our comprehension—so we must pray for "the spirit of wisdom and of revelation" (Ephesians 1:17) that we "may have power to comprehend" (Ephesians 3:18); we must wait to "receive power when the Holy Spirit has come upon [us]; and [we] shall be [his] witnesses . . ." (Acts 1:8). The Greek word for the witnesses is *maturion,* from which our word "martyr" comes. We are called to a certain form of martyrdom, of torment and suffering when we are called to leap out of the confining, restricted skins of our little worlds of self-security, living behind walls like the wealthy of Calcutta, to identify with the whole world.

The growth of the church must be a witness and sign to the world of the growth of the cosmos toward completion and maturity, encouraging the total world enterprise to work toward that end, namely, the unity and reconciliation of all things.

5 Numerical Growth of the Church

It can be readily assumed that when the theme of church growth is mentioned, the instant perception of its meaning is in numerical terms. We are not so callous in our perception that we attribute ultimate value to bulk and size as further indication of our culture of "quantitative colossalism."[1] Unlike what Pliny stated regarding the post-Hellenic Roman culture, "Not being able to make our values beautiful, we make them huge,"[2] we, out of our genuine valuation placed on the frequency of converted people, hope for greater possibilities of a changed world. While we are inescapably part of a culture that places high value on numerical size and physical growth, and we tend to join the larger churches in a success-oriented society, I wish to assume that the basic impulse for numerical growth in a church is motivated more on basic theological grounds and less on social and cultural grounds. Simply to dispose of growth in church membership as a social phenomenon arising out of the American cultural drive for success and achievement seems less than fair and generous.

American church growth in membership reached its peak in the fifties and sixties of recent history, out of the convergence of suburban development and the widespread practice of visitation evangelism by the laity. The growth reached such phenomenal heights in suburban churches that church leaders became deeply concerned with their successes as possible signs of neutralization of the cost of discipleship. Since those years a decided decline has set in, as these communities surrendered their highly protected homogeneous character and diversified urban characteristics began to prevail.

I

One of the great ironies of history is that church growth, in the immediate context of American history, has occurred in homogeneous segregated societies and declined in diversified open societies. The great churches of our urban centers prospered while cities protected the village character of a dominant ruling people, with small marginal minorities; as long as cities remained centers of white dominance, if not white supremacy, churches grew. But when the social milieu began to reflect the gospel mandate of the unity of the human family—an open society in which there are no minorities but all are members of one majority, a society in which housing and playgrounds, jobs and education, clubs and restaurants are equally available to all people—strangely, even if temporarily, churches began to decline.

Perhaps, in the providence of God, this phenomenon speaks loudly and clearly that God's ultimate concern is not the salvaging and preservation of the church but the saving and redeeming of the world; that God's ultimate concern is not the success of the church but the salvation of the world, for which the church exists as means, agent, and instrument. He is more concerned, for example, that New York City become an open society than he is that churches are opened; that a human community of equality and reciprocity become real than there be crowded congregations of middle-class white Americans. He is more concerned that the large army of unemployed become disbanded into jobs of challenging employment than he is for the leading citizens to be charter members of the Fifth Avenue and Park Avenue churches. In the plan and purpose of God, his church is subordinate, the world is primary; the church is the means and the world is the end; the church exists only for one purpose: to minister to the world. "God is concerned about the world," says Hendrik Kraemer. "In all that has happened in Christ, the whole of mankind is in God's view. The Church is provisional, not definitive. Consequently, the Church does not primarily exist on behalf of itself, but on behalf of the world."[3] These words are unforgettable. Therefore, our concern should primarily be not the growth or decline of the church, but the growth or decline of New York City, of Boston, of the U.S.A. What's happening to our nation and world should be the number one agenda in our churches. A robust church in the middle of a decaying city is nothing to be proud of; it is much better to have a declining church in the midst of a robust city. The health of the city, of our world, is God's primary agenda, for which the church exists as means and instrument. To state it in ultimate terms: the final mark of the church's success is to affect the world in such a way that the church works itself out of its job and makes itself unnecessary, like the foreign missionary who does her job so well in affirming and supporting the nationals in their leadership that she becomes unnecessary, or like parents whose role is fulfilled so commendably that they no longer become needed props for children who have grown into responsible individuals.

So the role of the church is to rejoice when the world grows up—when it takes over the care of the indigent, the support of the widow and the orphan, the education of children; when it gives shelter to the homeless and aid to unmarried mothers. There was a time in our nation's history when the church assumed these ministries and found great meaning and purpose in its role of being so needed. Surrendering these roles has not been easy; the church has felt somewhat like the mother experiencing withdrawal pains when her children leave home and she feels unnecessary. The church should rejoice that what began as the widow's mite of the Deacons' Fund administered only to the few has now become available to all needy persons, because the world has grown up and is administering its public welfare funds. The church should be proud and be glad that its insistence and will for the education of children and youth, and toward that end built its schools at great cost, has now resulted in universal education through the public schools and mass higher education through the state universities. Also, hospitals and clinics, trade schools and recreational facilities, and the medical and educational institutions around the world were often started by the Christian missionary movement. The whole independence movement, throwing off the yoke of foreign imperialism, found its seminal germination in the hearts and minds of men and women touched by the gospel brought by the missionaries. So if there is a decline in missionary personnel, let's rejoice that in many parts of the world their declining need is often tribute to the effectiveness of their contribution; the national churches have grown up into responsible independence, and the nations have grown up in so many ways to assume responsibilities the churches started.

The role of the church is the role of an inconspicuous enabler; its deeds should be largely invisible to the public eye like salt and leaven, taking on more of what we currently understand as the female principle of invisible strength than the masculine principle of apparent strength, more substance, less theater. It is interesting to note that our Lord has warned: "And when you pray, you must not be like the hypocrites; for they love to stand and pray in the synagogues and at the street corners, that they may be seen by men . . ." (Matthew 6:5). The word "hypocrite" comes from the Greek word *hupocrites*, meaning a stage actor or impersonator, and the word "be seen" in the Greek text is *theathenai*, from which our word "theater" comes. Don't be a theatrical stage actor and play to the galleries of the world. The church's role is invisible substance, not theater! The church regards itself as dispensable for the sake of a world that is indispensable; its role is "to be spent," writes Hans-Ruedi Weber, "which is part of the sacrificial terminology and means literally 'to be poured out as libation'"[4] (Philippians 2:17; 2 Timothy 4:6). "That I may know him . . . and the fellowship of his sufferings . . . ," writes Paul (Philippians 3:10, KJV) and again: "Now I rejoice in my sufferings for your sake, and in my flesh I complete what is lacking in Christ's afflictions for the sake of his body . . . the church" (Colossians 1:24).

It appears that the primary role of the church in relation to the world is suffering, even as "the heart of the gospel" is revealed as "the pain of God," in the words of the Japanese theologian Kitamori;[5] or it is like Kierkegaard's description of a poet: "an unhappy creature, whose heart is tortured by deepest suffering, but whose lips are so formed that when his sighs and cries stream out over them, their sound becomes like the sound of beautiful music."[6]

Sharing in the sufferings of Christ for the world; bearing the sins of the world, our sins of Vietnam; carrying the guilt and condemnation of the world, the guilt of racism, and the guilt of national arrogance; becoming the world's scapegoat; accepting the blame for excessive materialism and exorbitant consumption of diminishing resources without demand for self-justification; suffering in silence in bearing the sins of many; engaging in an outrageous act—to "love your enemies, bless them that curse you, do good to them that hate you, and pray for them which despitefully use you, and persecute you" (Matthew 5:44, KJV)—involve pain and suffering, the lonely austerity of the cross, the silent vigil of midnight, and the dreadful forsakenness of the desert. I heard someone say to another: "What appeals to me about your face is the pain and suffering it reflects." That is a profound tribute, reminding us of the faces of Lincoln, Jeremiah, Roger Williams, Jonathan Edwards, Robert E. Lee, Mahatma Gandhi— faces with deep lines caused by suffering. George W. Truett, probably the greatest preacher the South produced, carried to his grave the tragedy of his accidental shooting of his hunting companion. Only the beseeching plea of his whole congregation prevented his surrendering the ministry; but the plaintive note of healing hope, always a mark of his preaching, is traced to that moment of unspeakable agony. "I am now ready to be offered, and the time of my departure is at hand. I have fought a good fight, I have finished my course, I have kept the faith" (2 Timothy 4:6-7, KJV). Paul made no attempt to protect his indispensability, to absolutize his importance, "to regard himself more highly than he ought to think"; he had a "sane view of himself" (Romans 12:3, Moffatt) as disposable, willing to accept death by way of corporate and institutional rejection and repudiation by martyrdom. Paul probably felt, "My preservation is of little concern to me, but the preservation of the world is my perennial concern." In fact, he actually said, "I could wish that I myself were accursed and cut off from Christ for the sake of my brethren, my kinsmen by race" (Romans 9:3).

II

Does the provisional nature of the church mean we can take on an attitude of indifference as to its numerical growth and size? Can we callously repudiate any interest in "The Book of Numbers" as the "numbers game," absolve ourselves from the responsibility of numerical growth, and dwell in the twilight of the self-induced assumption that smallness is necessarily beautiful? When smallness is the result of unfaithfulness, of the absence of concerned outreach, of lethargy and indifference and smug complacency, then the smallness is a judgment and an indictment.

The church must be as large in scope and breadth as necessary to be a sign and miniature model in history of the scope and breadth of the gospel and the ultimate nature of the universe. We have said that the ultimate end and purpose of church growth is the growth of the cosmos into final unity, with all contending divisions and alienations of life gathered up in a reconciling unity in Christ; and the church is a sign of hope of that promised goal.

Therefore the church must be large enough in its breadth and length to embrace representatives of the typical barriers and alienations of our contemporary history, to undergo the painful encounter of alienated people, separated people, divided people, and to pursue, find, and discover their God-given unity in Jesus Christ.

The largest numerical record of conversion and growth in the New Testament is found in Acts 2 when, in response to Peter's preaching at Pentecost, "there were added that day about three thousand souls" (Acts 2:41). What is most significant about those three thousand is that they represented "devout men from every nation under heaven. . . . Parthians and Medes and Elamites and residents of Mesopotamia, Judea and Cappadocia, Pontus and Asia, Phrygia and Pamphylia, Egypt and the parts of Libya belonging to Cyrene, and visitors from Rome, both Jews and proselytes, Cretans and Arabians, we hear them telling in our own tongues the mighty works of God" (Acts 2:5-11).

Since the gospel is for "every nation under heaven" and since its aim is "to unite all things in him, things in heaven and things on earth" (Ephesians 1:10), the church must be a sign of this hope, a provisional manifestation in history, a taste of the future already in the present (Psalm 34:8; 1 John 1:1-3).

When we speak of the missionary character of the church, we are speaking of this expulsive, explosive, universal drive and insistence, embracing the whole world, all the nations, all the families of earth; its imperializing affection; its total cosmic strategy, the whole world community taken over by the conquest of compassion in the power of the Spirit by the rule and reign of its rightful Lord and Sovereign. Thus our sending missionaries to the ends of the earth is a sign of the universal character of the gospel, that Jesus Christ is Lord for all humankind. In like manner also, every congregation is a reflection of the missionary impulse of the gospel, that in Christ "all" are made one, "all" are united, "all" are reconciled. That universal note is what the church is all about.

When people step into your church, what do they see? Do they see devout men and women from "every nation under heaven," every institution in society, every class, every political party, every economic interest; people separated by the distance and strangeness of alien tongues and philosophies, standards and values; people understanding through the mystery of grace, transcending even the barriers of language? The nation is often imperiled with a dead-locked strike, which in the case of one coal strike lasted more than seventy-five days, resulting in a "deteriorating energy outlook for the nine-state area centering on Ohio."[7] Here was a classic struggle between labor and management, represented by the United Mine Workers and the coal industry. The question we must face is: in the life of the church, in the life of a congregation, do we have both coal miners—sturdy, tough-minded men who spend their working years in the bowels of the earth, digging for coal that feeds the furnace of industry—and executive managers occupying the same pew, sharing the same Communion table, listening to the same Word, and responding in mutual penitence and obedience? The coal miner and the industrial executive are equally precious in the sight of God, in dignity, in worth, in character, in nobility; the two persons differ only in gifts, and these differing gifts are equally essential to the economy of God. The worth of a person, her or his value and contributions, is not determined by whether one is a blue-collar or a white-collar worker, but by whether one is a faithful worker of integrity and competence. In the maelstrom of church life, which freedom and equality affords, we can battle out differences in ideas of how to attain unity in Christ as a guaranteed reality, not a questionable possibility. Paul spoke of our being "sealed with the promised Holy Spirit, which is the guarantee of our inheritance until we acquire possession of it . . ." (Ephesians 1:13-14). What reassurance this is to the whole world of industry, to the tough world of the bargaining table of labor/management negotiations, that we live in a universe where mutual agreement and settlement of differences is a guaranteed possibility; and it is in the struggles within the life of the church that we become assured of this, God's "pledge" and promise (Ephesians 1:12-14, NEB).

The continuing search for peace in the Middle East has led to the development of an understandable resentment, carefully hidden from public view, of the enormous Jewish lobby, so powerful that the Democratic party and even the president can ill afford to alienate it. This resentment can so easily erupt into a virulent anti-Semitism which has plagued human history for so long. And anti-Semitism has wider implications than relations to Jews alone; it becomes a symbolic antipathy to all "undesirable" people. The New Testament defines the reconciliation between Jew and Gentile as having the kind of representative character of all reconciliations of all enmities; the historic fracture which prevailed between Jew and Gentile was of such profound structural nature as to trivialize all other alienations; but now in Christ it is permanently resolved: "that is, how the Gentiles are fellow heirs, members of the same body, and partakers of the promise in Christ Jesus through the gospel" (Ephesians 3:6). This was the miracle in history which arrested the attention of the callous Romans, Jews, and Gentiles, historic enemies: "by one Spirit . . . were all baptized into one body . . . and all were made to drink of one Spirit" (1 Corinthians 12:13).

Every generation has its own particular classification of Gentiles and Jews, people for whom we have developed a cultural, political, or social aversion and which we develop with a clear conscience; and each generation has developed its own refined equivalent of anti-Semitism, not crude nor overtly cruel but with the incipient powers of gradual destruction and the slow, quiet capacities of wearing out the self-esteem and dignity of people.

Isn't it amazing how even the finest people, generous people, who exercise a wide contour of affirmation, have a blacklist in their memories—people they cannot trust, whom they regard as obstacles to progress, about whom they become eloquent in their caricatures, and whose condemnation they express with a moral passion?

Some have it in for people of wealth and power; others are uncomfortable with the poor, not knowing how to relate to them without the discomfort of patronizing solicitation or contempt for their ineptitude. Many of the rich and powerful have been edged out of the church by the isolating effectiveness of a studied distance maintained, leaving them effectively lonely and isolated from the community. We tend to have a bias against the homely and the unattractive and place an undue premium on the attractive, so that researchers have found "that physically attractive people are perceived as more sensitive, kind, interesting, strong, poised, modest, sociable, sexually warm and responsive and outgoing."[8]

What would happen if every nation and institution under heaven were represented in your church, rich and poor, blue-collar and white-collar, Jews and Gentiles, religious and irreligious, pious and impious, blacks and whites, Asians and Hispanics, Japanese industrialists and American steelworkers, Arabs and Jews, Russians and Chinese, French and Italians, South Koreans and Vietnamese; what if your church belonged to all people from all the institutions and classes and nations of the world? You would have a sizable church!

6 Reflective Growth of the Church

Americans pride themselves as being people of action, and impatient with reflection. We have stripped mountains of their forests with little reflection on the consequence of our atrocities. We have rapidly built our highways and bridges with little thought of their impending obsolescence in a few short years. We have recklessly sprayed the countryside with chemical pesticides without contemplating the poisoning of our rivers and lakes and the eventual death of our precious marine life. We produce automobiles with efficient abandon, with no serious thought and reflection as to the eventual poisoning of our atmosphere, threatening the health of our civilization. We acted with typical American decisiveness, dropping millions of tons of bombs in Vietnam without premeditation on the permanent scars to be left in that tiny, helpless nation, let alone the death and crippling of millions of its people. When we pride ourselves as being people of action, and impatiently brush aside our task of reflection and contemplation, we find ourselves contributing to a dangerous planet sweeping through space, unguided by moral direction, propelled by the collective will for movement and speed, enthralled by every achievement of velocity, without any serious questioning as to purpose of this frenetic action.

America can be a threat to the future because she has become the most powerful nation in the world without being the most thoughtful nation in the world to guide her power into constructive channels of hope. The sense of helplessness that prevails among our people, especially among the young, is a serious indictment of the crisis in which we find ourselves. Therefore when we speak of the need of the reflective growth of the church, we are speaking of something of critical importance, affecting the future of the cosmos.

I

It is no wonder that the Bible places such urgency on "wisdom" and "knowledge," "enlightenment" and the imperative necessity "to know" and to possess the power of comprehension. "I pray that the God of our Lord Jesus Christ, the all-glorious Father, may give you the spiritual powers of wisdom and vision, by which there comes the knowledge of him. I pray that your inward eyes may be illumined, so that you may know what is the hope to which he calls you . . . ," writes Paul (Ephesians 1:17-18, NEB). And again Paul prays and implores that you "may have power to comprehend with all the saints what is the breadth and length and height and depth, and to know the love of Christ which surpasses knowledge, that you may be filled with all the fulness of God" (Ephesians 3:18-19). Why do we need reflective powers, powers of comprehension, wisdom, and knowledge? "That you may know what is the hope to which he has called you, what are the riches of his glorious inheritance in the saints, and what is the immeasurable greatness of his power . . ." (Ephesians 1:18-19); ". . . what is the breadth and length and height and depth, and to know the love of Christ which surpasses knowledge, that you may be filled with all the fulness of God" (Ephesians 3:18-19).

The great black singer Roland Hayes, struggling against impossible odds to make his way in a world structured to resist his freedom to prove his enormous worth as a singer, was constantly reminded by his mother, "Remember who you are." We are all people of inherited wealth, wealth of unlimited possibilities and hope, wealth of immediate availability and currency we can appropriate today, wealth in the form of power comparable to the power that raised Jesus Christ from the dead, resurrection power. Most of us are unlike Roland Hayes; we forget who we really are, deny our worth, or go through life unaware, not comprehending "the riches of our inheritance," without even remotely reflecting on "the immeasurable greatness of his power in us"; rather we live in a state of confessed impoverishment, with a deep sense of our lack of adequacy, with little sense of power but the absense of power, with little sense of riches but an enormous sense of poverty, more acutely conscious of our deficiency than we are of our possessions. From time to time we read of pathetic creatures, with wealth tucked away in their cupboards, who live like misers, half-starved and without the comforts of home. And this is the way it is today.

We are a people who have lost the capacity to reflect on the deep things of God, to develop the powers of comprehension of the full sweep of human life, beginning, continuation, and consummation. "Finally, brethren, whatever is true, whatever is honorable, whatever is just, whatever is pure, whatever is lovely, whatever is gracious, if there is any excellence, if there is anything worthy of praise, think about these things" (Philippians 4:8). We must learn to think! We must love God not only with our hearts and souls but also with our minds, for we are "transformed by the renewal of [our] mind" (Romans 12:2).

II

It's no wonder that our Lord spent so much of his precious time within his brief three and one-half years' ministry in teaching his disciples. "Seeing the crowds, he went up on the mountain, and when he sat down his disciples came to him. And he opened his mouth and taught them" (Matthew 5:1-2). For the redemption of the world he often forsook the crowds and sought mountain retreats and other solitary spots to teach his disciples. What magnificent teaching that was as he sat on one end of the log and the disciples on the other end! Some of those lessons and lectures are preserved and speak to us today in the form and power of the Sermon on the Mount. Even Gandhi, a non-Christian, found these lessons compelling for his vision and pursuit of the national building of a new India. In the purpose of God, human life and human culture "grow up in every way into him who is the head, into Christ" (Ephesians 4:15), through meditation and reflection, through learning and listening, thinking and ruminating like the Hebrew psalmist whose

> . . . delight is in the law of the Lord,
>   and on his law he meditates day and night.
> He is like a tree
>   planted by streams of water,
> that yields its fruit in its season,

and its leaf does not wither.
In all that he does, he prospers.
—Psalm 1:2-3

Is it any wonder that our greatest music and art and our greatest literature also have emerged out of minds and hearts that have reflected deeply on the Word of God? Some time ago, eight hundred people met in Los Angeles in a Congress of the Laity "to discuss the religious and social issues of the day," and, according to James Reston who himself was one of the speakers,

> the idea behind the congress was that religion was too serious to be left to the clergy alone, and that social questions were too important to be left to political leaders. The congress felt the people themselves must get more deeply involved in the spiritual and material conflicts of the nation.[1]

Just a few days before Reston's comments, Edward Fiske had reported:

> Courses on ethics, once confined largely to departments of theology and philosophy, have moved into the mainstream of American universities and professional schools.
> At least half of the country's 116 medical schools, or about triple the number of five years ago, now have humanities departments or regular programs in medical ethics, and a similar trend is evident in law, engineering, public policy and other professional schools.[2]

As encouraging as these events are, they do not go far enough. I pray the day may come when not only the world's greatest art and music and literature once again emerge out of the spiritual powers of wisdom and vision but also that every science of human enterprise, be it economics, politics, medicine, or the law, become vocational expressions of the profound meaning of divine calling. Ethics is the pattern and style of human behavior in relation to God, neighbor, and nature, and this is the central quest and character of the human enterprise, which is the meaning of salvation. But the crucial issue and crisis today is institutional ethics,[3] how organizations and corporations behave in obedience and devotion to God, how "to do justice, and to love kindness and to walk humbly with your God" (Micah 6:8), how to act toward humankind and hold in reverence and awe the beauty and sanctity of nature. How desperately we need new pioneers in economic thought, arising out of the deepest insights of biblical materialism, rooted in Hebrew and Christian thought, intellectuals and thinkers to change the economic landscape of history! Think of the power that has been exerted by capitalism and Marxism, revolutionary ideas that have virtually shaped the history of the world for the last two hundred years.[4]

Christian thought provided the intellectual framework for Europe for a thousand years.[5] The church must now produce great pioneers in thought, who will create the new intellectual frame of reference for the next thousand years; within this framework a new economics, a new politics, new law, and new medicine can arise. If, in the purpose of God, his new order demands a "renewal of the mind," "eyes of the heart enlightened," "a new spirit of wisdom," and "new powers of comprehension," then the church is under an imperative mandate by election and calling to think, to explore, to engage in the most disciplined habit of reflection to pursue "the breadth and length and height and depth" of reality.

We should pray that God will raise up thinkers from our midst, contemporary models of Augustine, Thomas Aquinas, Martin Luther, Jonathan Edwards—men and women who will lead our world out of the morass and wilderness of our twentieth-century bondage into a new Exodus. China has had its Mao to lead that nation of 800 million into a new order. Marx has changed the world's map. Let us pray that God may raise up formative thinkers to reshape the contours of our culture toward God's new age.

III

What does this mean to us in the meantime? What can we do to encourage this kind of possibility? Think great thoughts, by which I mean, think eschatologically; think always in terms of the ultimate goal and purpose of history, the final end by which we decide on means. The great American economist Alfred Marshall is quoted by John Kenneth Galbraith: "The economist, like everyone else, must concern himself with the ultimate aims of man."[6] We are created to think great thoughts, to discern our common life in the light of eternity, to sense the meaning of life in the wide context of beginning and end, so that we measure the present against the backdrop of "In the beginning God" (Genesis 1:1) and "Then I saw a new heaven and a new earth" (Revelation 21:1). Someone has said our view of God is too small. Surely our view of life is too small, be it typically midwestern or southern, or eastern or western. We are not only parochial and regional but also narrowly contemporary, and we take pride in our contemporaneity as though this were a mark of an open mind living in the full face of reality. We are so narrowly restricted to the present, and the present provides no clue of purpose and meaning; only the future and the final future of God, the end and consummation of history, can provide that clue. We are living in a truncated piece of history, severed from the past and unillumined by the future; we give little praise to our antecedents and forebears, as being a part of the primitive and unenlightened past, without the advantages and achievements of the modern world, whatever they are.

Modernity is equated with wisdom; and the past, even the immediate past, is equated with ignorance. We are too busily consumed with the present to worry about the future; our immediate welfare is of such overriding concern, we have no surplus leisure to worry about the future of our country or planet. And yet that future stands in judgment on the present; it's that future that convicts and torments us, that brings disquiet within us (Psalm 42:5), because to live unaware of that future, or in conflict and contradiction to that future, is to go aginst the grain of the universe and to engage in the assault of self-destruction.

Toyohiko Kagawa, the great Christian leader from Japan, was once being severely criticized by some professors of the University of Southern California when Professor Taylor of the Department of Religion rose in defense of the visitor from across the water and said, "Perhaps we cannot fully appreciate what Dr. Kagawa has said today because he moves in a different orbit; he moves in the orbit of God." It's that "breadth and length and height and depth" of God's orbit and time that provides space enough for human breadth and movement, enough for human purpose and meaning.

Did it take Watergate to raise a warning signal about the crassness of the legal profession, of every profession, of politics and government, of business and industry, bereft of reflection and thought and contemplation of end and purpose of life? Is this the reason why professional schools are introducing courses in ethics and studies in the humanities? Watergate is simply a tip of the iceberg, and the chastening effects are still in question. The public is still afflicted with yet another lucrative publication, profit out of the scandal of Watergate, about which James Reston comments: "H. R. Haldeman is still proving that it pays to be loyal to nobody, even to the truth, even to yourself, but everybody's on to him now, since his commercial success is even more repulsive than his political failure."[7]

To search the Scriptures, to meditate on his Law day and night and hide his word in our hearts (Psalm 119:11), and "beginning with Moses and all the prophets" to have the Scriptures interpreted concerning Jesus Christ (Luke 24:27) becomes an imperative calling of every Christian. The world is perishing for the lack of a philosophy of history. The Bible and the Christian faith are basically a clue and treatise on the meaning and purpose of human history. Therefore the church is called by God to be philosophers and theologians, interpreters of the signs of the times, futurists speaking to the future of the human enterprise. When I first met the great Karl Barth, the greatest theologian of our day, I was surprisingly impressed with his statement that every Christian must be a theologian who should think out as succinctly as possible his faith in Jesus Christ. You cannot absolve yourself by relying on your ministers to be your theologians; we must all be philosophers and theologians because the greatest need of our world today is to know why we are here and where we are going. Paul in Athens, the center of world culture, after preaching "Jesus and the resurrection" at the Areopagus, was questioned by the Epicurean and Stoic philosophers: "We wish to know therefore what these things mean" (Acts 17:20). The great question facing the human family today is the question of meaning—the meaning of life, the meaning of history, the meaning of the cosmos. In illuminating that meaning, one brings light to a world of darkness. For indeed, "You are the light of the world. A city set on a hill cannot be hid. Nor do men light a lamp and put it under a bushel, but on a stand, and it gives light to all in the house. Let your light so shine before men, that they may see good works and give glory to your Father who is in heaven" (Matthew 5:14-16).

7

Organic Growth of the Church

Once in each of the last three centuries America has faced a time of trial, a time of testing so severe that not only the form but even the existence of our nation have been called in question. Born out of the revolutionary crisis of the Atlantic world in the late 18th century, America's first time of trial was our struggle for independence and the institution of liberty. The second time of trial came not long before the end of the nation's first hundred years. At stake was the preservation of the union and the extension of equal protection of the laws to all members of society. We live at present in a third time of trial at least as severe as those of the Revolution and the Civil War. It is a test whether our inherited institutions can be creatively adapted to meet the 20th-century crisis of justice and order at home and in the world. It is a test of whether republican liberty established in a remote agrarian backwater of the world in the 18th century shall prove able or willing to confront successfully the age of mass society and international revolution. It is a test of whether we can control the very economic and technical forces, which are our greatest achievement, before they destroy us.[1]

These are the prophetic words of Robert Bellah, summoning American conscience to face the "third time of trial" in our nation's history, the crisis of our inherited institutions. No wonder we are faced today with a plethora of restructuring in government, business, education, and even in the church. Every denomination in the last decade has reorganized and restructured, absorbing an inordinate amount of its resources and strength. The World

53

Council of Churches' Study on the Missionary Structure of the Congregation was noted by the late Chairman of the Central Committee, Franklin Fry, as the most rewarding study conducted by the Council. The wave of organizational development that swept our culture and the longing anticipation for the emergence of a new economics and a new politics are dramatic symptoms of the cruciality of the corporate and collective nature of life, so that if human life is to be renewed and transformed, it must be changed corporately and organically. Thus, we can see the need of organic growth of the church.

I

We are unfortunately steeped in the tradition of individualism, especially in religion, so that Christian faith is understood to be primarily a personal, individual, and private matter. Therefore at the rite of baptism, the candidate is asked, "Do you believe in Jesus Christ as your personal Savior?" We should also be asking the congregation, "Do you covenant to love and affirm him or her as a member of the body?" Therefore the baptism occurring in the presence of the congregation, in which all participate and share, is as essential as the personal confession of the candidate. The personal act and the collective act cannot be separated; the one is not prior to the other. There is no possibility of a personal faith and a personal decision apart from a corporate and collective faith and decision; the gospel comes to the individual through the church, so the personal meaning of salvation would be vacuous apart from the corporate nature of salvation. Therefore, at this moment in history, under the spell of a new form of individualism, of the human potential movement, fueled by its oversimplification of religion and psychiatry, we must recover the social and corporate nature of reality. Would it be unfair to say that so much of our reliance on counseling and the desperate need to discern our self-identity arise out of the erosion of community, a diminished sense of family, the disappearance of neighborhood, and the gradual dissipation of the social chemistry which coagulates and coheres community?

Biblical history predated European and American individualism. The Old Testament's unit of reality is a particular people, Israel, and even when individuals loom in importance, they emerge as representatives of a larger entity; Adam is understood, in the words of H. Wheeler Robinson, as "a corporate personality"; Abraham is a representative person of "all the families of the earth." The New Testament story is again the drama of a people, a people of God, the church, called into covenant with Jesus Christ. Our Lord left a single legacy, a people, a group of disciples, through whom he continued his mission of redemption. The letters of Paul are the admonishing of a people, teachings on how a people should respond to the call and initiative of Jesus Christ.

How to act as a body, then, is a most serious issue which faces history. How we act together is our supreme responsibility, and personal action is important in relation to, and not in isolation from, it. "For as in one body we have many members, and all the members do not have the same function, so we, though many, are one body in Christ, and individually members one of another" (Romans 12:4-5). The whole twelfth chapter of Romans, which deals with the meaning of response to the grace of God and is stated in social and corporate terms, contains clues to a social organism: "teaching," "exhortation," "liberality," "aid," "acts of mercy," "love one another with brotherly affection," "outdo one another in showing honor," "contribute to the needs of the saints, practice hospitality," "do not be haughty," "live peaceably with all" (see Romans 12:7-18). These are things one cannot do alone.

In the classic chapter, 1 Corinthians 12, we again have Paul dealing with the organic nature of reality reflected in the church. "For just as the body is one and has many members, and all the members of the body, though many, are one body, so it is with Christ. For by one Spirit we were all baptized into one body—Jews or Gentiles, slaves or free—and all were made to drink of one Spirit" (1 Corinthians 12:12-13). This leads us to suggest that God's primary concern is the creation of a people, in anticipation of his ultimate concern for the creation of a cosmos. We must be extricated out of our self-obsession that the universe exists for us, with us as the center. We are like the child who, waking out of his sleep, looking out of the window, and seeing his mother chatting with other people, is shocked to think that she has a life also, apart from him. Can we grow out of our extended childishness; can we abandon the assumption that the universe exists for our welfare; can we change the way we accept or reject anything based on what it does or does not do for us? Most of us now choose jobs or professions, choose communities or friends, select churches or clubs, based on what they can do for us and our families.

The picture of Edenic paradise is a picture of communion between man and woman, in harmony with nature, unmolested and uninhibited by the alien spirit of sin, not man or woman in lonely grandeur, as though the creation of a superb human or an incredibly beautiful creature or the shaping of a human genius were God's ultimate purpose. "Let us make man in our image, after our likeness" (Genesis 1:26). Even God in reference to himself speaks collectively: "Let us make man in our image" (Genesis 1:26) as though the triune God abhors individual solitude and covets fellowship and communion. "It is not good that the man should be alone; I will make him a helper fit for him" (Genesis 2:18). What began in the Garden of Eden will culminate in a city, the "holy city, new Jerusalem, coming down out of heaven from God" (Revelation 21:2). No names are mentioned, no roll call anticipated, simply that "He will dwell with them, and they shall be his people, and God himself will be with them" (Revelation 21:3).

Thus, how to be a people must be our primary concern. "You are a chosen race, a royal priesthood, a holy nation, God's own people, that you may declare the wonderful deeds of him who called you out of darkness into his marvelous light. Once you were no people but now you are God's people" (1 Peter 2:9-10).

II

Therefore, institutionalization, organization, and politics are so essential. What is politics but the science of the "polis" or the city, how human civilization is ordered and managed in an urban collectivity? We must shed the dreadful assumption that the gospel deals only with the human heart and not with human commerce. How the human community lives out its ordered life is at the heart of the gospel.

What is the meaning of salvation? Its roots are found in the Old Testament concept of "shalom" meaning "wholeness, integrity, Heil, the state of complete integration of a community, its restoration into its original God-willed design," writes Hendrik Kraemer.[2] H. Richard Niebuhr would state the meaning of salvation or the goal of the church as the "*increase among men of the love of God and neighbor.*"[3] Therefore when we claim salvation in Jesus Christ, we are reclaiming "the original God-willed design" of "complete integration of a community," of a loving society as existed between man and woman in the Garden, in love with God, with each other, and with nature. That is true salvation.

Therefore, let us cease talking about the social implications of the gospel when we deal with the institutional issues. How we live out our ordered life as a human social community, as a family, as a school, as a business, as a state and government, as a nation, in obedient relation to the sovereign God, in loving relation to neighbor, and in harmony with the natural environment is an essential part of the gospel.

Therefore the purpose of the church is to provide in history clues of organic life, what it means to be a society of people. In recent years, we have relied heavily on the business model to reorganize our churches; church executives go to Harvard Business School to learn the norms of efficiency. Without implying God cannot speak through the Harvard Business School, I must emphasize that the church cannot evade the God-given responsibility to model and remodel new shapes of institutional organic life, which reflect God's purpose of human salvation and shalom, dismantling every structure which results in human tyranny. The repression of human rights in the apartheid structure of South Africa is a dramatic symbolization of the urgency of institutional conversion. There are many converted persons in South Africa, persons of impeccable character. But South Africa needs a radical change in its collective life, in its political, economic, and religious order; it needs to dismantle its apartheid structure and shape a new social order to manifest the saving grace of Jesus Christ our Lord.

III

How then can we grow organically, so that our institutional life reflects God's purpose of human salvation, knowing that structure, far from being a neutral quotient, a morally neutral encasement of human society, is as determinative as substance? An apartheid structure containing moral people results in apartheid society. A racist institution containing moral people results in a racist society.

For one thing, we must develop a theology of institutions, by which we mean an understanding of God's calling and God's expectations of institutions, and therefore the accountability of institutions before God. We have, unfortunately, in the history of the church abstracted personal accountability before God; "What must I do to be saved?" The current revival of the "born again" experience is a new symptom of the hunger for personal experience of forgiveness and new life. My own conversion came at age sixteen, an event which changed the course of my life. I would covet seeing young people in our churches come to a moment of decisive decision. But that's only one part of the gospel mandate to be kept in tension with God's expectation of "a people," "a nation." The Great Commission calls for the discipling "of all nations" (Matthew 28:19). And in the final consummation "many nations shall come" to "the mountain of the house of the Lord" (see Micah 4:1-2); and in the final judgment, "before him will be gathered all the nations, and he will separate them one from another . . ." (Matthew 25:32). Paul's question on the Damascus Road, "What shall I do, Lord?" (Acts 22:10), must also become the collective question out of the crisis of our collective behavior: "What shall we do, Lord?"

Then, if institutional behavior is as crucial as personal behavior, and institutional accountability to God is as urgent as personal obedience to him, the ministry of the gospel toward institutional change and birth of new styles of collective life must become the ministry of the lay apostles, the lay communicants, the lay evangelists, the lay theologians, and the lay ministerium. The contemporary clergy largely ministers to the world of private and familial hurts and seeks to mediate the grace of God to the healing of those afflictions. But the world of the public arena, the stormy world of commerce, the crisis of government, and the uncertain ominous calm of the world of education, and the rest are the worlds, the social milieu, the habitation of the laity, who daily suffer in their agony or celebrate in their glory, who are responsible for the radical redesigning of these outmoded and obsolete structures which have lost their innate capacity to carry the freight of human commerce and industry.

Aren't the American railroads a paradigm of the institutional obsolescence implicit in all of our collective, corporate enterprise? For a nation of unparalleled wealth, resources, technology, and people to admit such collective ineptitudes as the urban deterioration of Detroit or the fiscal disaster of New York City is a sign of a widespread need in bringing together the collective resources of our nation toward discerning and shaping new styles of corporate responsibility through the renewal and reforming and redoing of our institutions. And the church must reorder its organic life as a witness and sign of hope for the world.

8
Growth in Transformative Impact

What plagued Israel plagues the church: the assumption that they alone are God's people. Israel again and again assumed that they alone were heirs of God's salvation and Gentiles were outside the realm of God's grace. The very notion of Gentiles was a notion of godlessness, separation, and alienation, outside the common-wealth of God. Israel unfortunately found meaning and purpose in their sense of closeness while the Gentile world suffered rejection and separation from the purpose of God.

This kind of introversion and incredible complacency pre-vails among many Christian people today and too often provides the motivating impulse for mission and evangelism. There is enormous power residing in the assumption that only the church, only Christians who confess Jesus Christ as Lord and Savior, are in the realm of salvation and redemption, and all others are in the realm of damnation. Therefore, the driving missionary impulse would be to win as many into the church as possible, for only in the church and as the church are we assured God's promise of everlasting life. Viewed from this perspective, we live in a tragic world, with little islands of hope represented in the churches in a vast ocean of hopelessness. Noah's ark then becomes our paradigm and model of understanding, the desperate effort of salvaging what we can before the final floods of judgment. For those who are rescued, it gives enormous satisfaction, or does it? Would you wish to be part of a universe in which the vast majority perish and a small remnant survives? Can you conceive of a world under the waters of judgment, with a single ark of survival?

Israel and the church remember the dramatic story of the flood and the ark; they forget that "the waters had subsided from the face of the ground" (Genesis 8:8); "the waters were dried from off the earth" (Genesis 8:13); and that God made an everlasting covenant with the whole world, "'that never again shall all flesh be cut off by the waters of a flood, and never again shall there be a flood to destroy the earth.' And God said, 'This is the sign of the covenant which I make between me and you and every living creature that is with you, for all future generations'" (Genesis 9:11-12).

I

That little handful of despairing disciples also thought that they alone among all the peoples of earth belonged to Christ. Their sense of a helpless minority is expressed in the plaintive note of disappointment: "But we had hoped he was the one to redeem Israel. Yes, and besides all this, it is now the third day since this happened" (Luke 24:21). They were unaware that they were speaking to the risen Lord, except they sensed something new: "Did not our hearts burn within us, while he talked to us on the road, while he opened to us the scriptures?" (Luke 24:32). Yes, something new had happened: cosmos with a new beginning, like the dawn of creation when chaos was turned into order, and out of nothing, something, light shining in the darkness that the darkness could not overcome, the first signs of the new creation, the setting into motion the growth and emergence of the ultimate kindgom of God.

A coronation had taken place or, in the words of Professor O. Michel, "enthronement."[1] "All authority in heaven and on earth has been given to me," said Jesus (Matthew 28:18). He knew that his hearers lived with the hope of the coming of "one like a son of man" spoken by Daniel: "And to him was given dominion and glory and kingdom, that all peoples, nations, and languages should serve him . . ." (Daniel 7:13-14).[2] What centuries of hope had anticipated was now fulfilled. A new world order has come into being in which Jesus Christ is declared Lord and Sovereign, not simply over Israel and the church but over "all peoples, nations, and languages," an order in which they all are accountable to Jesus Christ, even as the church is accountable to him.

President Sadat and the Egyptian nation, since the enthronement event of the resurrection, owe their ultimate allegiance to
Jesus Christ, despite their claim to be Muslims. Prime Minister
Begin and the Israeli people who await the coming of the Messiah
will discern to their amazement that the Messiah of their hope is
the same Lord who has already come, that the Jesus of Bethlehem,
Christ of the cross and resurrection, is in fact the Messiah of Jewish
hope.

Some time back, the president threatened to invoke the com-
pulsory back-to-work procedure of the Taft-Hartley Act. But let
it be known that the President of the U.S.A., the 160,000 members
of the United Mine Workers Union, and the coal industry itself, all
stand under the judgment of a higher law, the ultimate authority of
Jesus Christ. While the balance of power between the political,
popular, and economic institutions resulted in a stalemate, there is
no negotiating from a position of equal power with the authority
of Christ. He alone is supreme. His Word is law. His will is
ultimate good. To seek his mind is what the negotiation demands.
The pursuit of peace in the Middle East is a pursuit of the
conscience of the universe, the mind of Jesus Christ.

What is notable since the resurrection of Jesus Christ is the
universalizing of the gospel, by which we mean that the totality of
reality and the full scope of the universe come under the rule and
reign of Christ. In one sense Christ has always been "heir of all
things, through whom also he created the world," according to
Hebrews (Hebrews 1:2), and "all things were created through him
and for him," according to Colossians (Colossians 1:16). What has
been a hidden secret, however, is now made public; what has been
implicit is now made explicit; what has been true from everlasting
to everlasting is now made manifest in time and space and history.
That is the meaning of the incarnation. There has always been an
eternal cross, but it was made manifest in the cross of Christ.[3]
Christ has always borne the right of lordship, by his acts of creation
and redemption. But the resurrection of Jesus Christ became the
public event of declaration and proclamation to all "principalities
and powers," to all "peoples, nations, and languages," of the
actual, historical, lordship of Jesus Christ over the whole world.

The resurrection of Christ was no mere warning, advance
warning, of the imminence, the impending possibility of his
assertion of power and dominion in order that the nations would
eventually accept and come to terms with his lordship. Rather, it
was a declaration of an immediate reality, a political fact, a

pragmatic reality, actual change in the administration of the cosmos. What had been a debated and embattled claim to authority and supremacy, in which power and the seizure of power vacillated, was now settled; no change in authority would any longer be possible; Jesus Christ would remain as the established Lord of the cosmos.

Therefore the resurrection of Christ is the flag-raising event for all the nations of earth to see and to hear who is the center of world authority and power. That's the reason, in Matthew 28:18-19, that the declaration of Christ's authority, "all authority in heaven and on earth is given to me," is immediately followed by the missionary charge to "go therefore and make disciples of all nations" (Matthew 28:19); and the central nature of that charge is public declaration of the authority of Jesus Christ over all the nations. Therefore the heart of the gospel is proclaiming "the imperious Lord" of the world and is calling all peoples, nations, and languages to love, obey, and follow the authority of its acknowledged Lord.

II

The resurrection of Jesus Christ is the public declaration of his supreme, "imperious lordship" over the world, in the words of John Mackay; it is also the declaration of the ultimate resurrection of the whole cosmos. "For as in Adam all die, so also in Christ shall all be made alive" (1 Corinthians 15:22). "But in fact Christ has been raised from the dead, the first fruits of those who have fallen asleep" (1 Corinthians 15:20). So with the resurrection of our Lord began, as first fruit, the anticipatory promise of the total resurrection of the cosmos. We live in a universe, in a world, in which the "powers of the endless life," resurrection power, are already operative like leaven and seed and salt, so that what Christ as Lord expects and demands of the nations, in obedience and accountability, are reasonable demands, demands for which new moral and spiritual resources are amply available, demands which give fulfillment and meaning.

Why was President Nixon able to begin negotiations with Chairman Mao Tse-tung and Prime Minister Chou En-lai? Because we live in a world in which the fundamental nature of reality is unity and reconciliation, because while the waves of history rise and fall with the winds of change, in the silent depths of the ocean of reality, the nature of the universe has begun to change toward ultimate unity and reconciliation. "To live in accord with the deeper rhythm might be to ignore the surface rhythm of life," writes John Dunne.[4] Ever since the coronation of Christ's lordship over the world, the basic nature of the world has changed and is changing from despair to hope, from ultimate death to ultimate life (1 Corinthians 15:22), from the passing of the old to the emergence of the new creation (2 Corinthians 5:17); the old order is passing away and the new order is begun.

To visit in a home and be inspired and renewed and cleansed with an overwhelming sense of goodness personified is a sign of the new order of things. To go to minister to one suffering from a long-term illness, facing the possibility of the end with equanimity and fearlessness, with confidence and hope, so that the one who attempts to minister is ministered unto, is also triumphant evidence that we are living in a new day of hope and promise. To spend an evening with a couple, who by profession and achievement are considered by society as social elites, demonstrating a life of genuine humility and graciousness is a clue that we live in the new and final days looking toward the consummation of history.

We live in a world being transformed by the power and authority of Christ, not a world doomed to destruction, but a world ruled and managed by Jesus Christ; it is disobedient and defiant, to be sure, but no defiance can successfully prevent and frustrate Christ's sovereign rule and the fulfillment of his purpose.

III

Then, how about the church's growth in transformative impact? What happens to the whole world is the end and purpose of the gospel, and the church exists as an instrument to that end. That the whole world, the whole cosmos, be renewed, redeemed, transformed, and become "a new heaven and new earth" is the purpose of God and his goal for history. And the church exists to serve God and the world to that end. The church's role is to proclaim to the world what has happened to the world. What has happened to the world? It has come under new ownership: "You do not belong to yourselves; you were bought at a price" (1 Corinthians 6:20, NEB). "There came one like a son of man . . . and to him was given dominion and glory and kingdom . . ." (Daniel 7:13). The church's supreme role is to proclaim to the world that "Christ rules as Lord." Therefore the whole world, all the nations of the world, and all peoples and institutions of the nations are accountable to Jesus Christ as Lord. He is Lord not only of

Christians and of the church, but also he is Lord over all. In the words of Oscar Cullmann, ". . . everything is created through Christ. . . . everything is reconciled through him. . . . everything is subjected to God, who is all in all."[5]

The church's role is to discern the nature of the world in the light of what God has done to the world, and to summon and persuade the world to become what it is called to be. "Go therefore and make disciples of all nations . . . teaching them . . ." (Matthew 28:19-20). The role of teaching is not basically transferring information from teacher to pupil, but discerning gifts and capabilities residing in the learner, evoking them to visibility and awareness, that these residual gifts and talents may be developed to the maximum and maturity. I owe so much to my grammar-school teacher, Miss Marjorie Trembath. I remember so little of what she taught me, but I cannot forget that she loved me, and believed in me, and saw possibilities of what I might become. The height of my aspiration rose no higher than to be a truckdriver, which I thought was the most exciting enterprise in the world! How well I remember her shaking her head with a look of disappointment and saying that I could do better than that! And when she said I could do better than that, something happened within me. I developed a new aspiration to become what I had not seen possible before. Elizabeth O'Connor, of the Church of the Saviour in Washington, D.C., writes that Gordon Cosby says "the primary task and primary mission of the Christian is to call forth the gifts of others." She quotes him:

> We are not sent into the world in order to make people good. We are not sent to encourage them to do their duty. . . . to impose new burdens on them, rather than calling forth the gift which is the essence of the person himself. . . . They can be what in their deepest hearts they know that they were intended to be, they can do what they were meant to do. As Christians, we are heralds of these good tidings.[6]

That is the role of midwifery of the church in relation to the world: to bring to birth, after long gestation and incubation, new ideas, new values, new realities, new concepts, new events, and new histories in the world. The world is pregnant with the kingdom of God; the new creation is forming in the womb and bosom of the cosmos; and the church must fulfill its tutorial function for the world to fulfill her destiny, to call forth the gifts residing in the world, to live up to its full potential, to discern its identity, to become who she really is and, in the words of David Tracy, to "[affirm] the ultimate significance and final worth of our lives, our thoughts, and actions, here and now, in nature and in history."[7]

The church cannot transform the world any more than the teacher can transform the pupil. But the church can precipitate and evoke that internal ferment and transformative process by proclaiming that "Christ rules as Lord," which creates "a crisis" in the world with the need to make a "decision," in the face of a new "discernment" of "judgment" and "good will," writes Arnold Come.[8]

Don't give up on the world! Have faith in it as possessing in the depth of its being hidden resources, subterranean streams and rivers of cleansing hope and renewing possibilities. It needs to be trusted and loved and affirmed, that this monstrous world, awkward and out of shape, disproportionately built, without balance and symmetry, without elegance and style, may grow in the symmetry of maturity and the elegance of the new creation. "God so loved the world that he gave his only Son" (John 3:16).

9 Growth in Unity

"That they may all be one; even as thou, Father, art in me, and I in thee, that they also may be in us, so that the world may believe that thou has sent me" (John 17:21). This is the heart of the prayer offered by our Lord just a few hours before his lonely vigil in Gethsemane, the desertion of his disciples, and his death by crucifixion. Words uttered and prayers offered in the final moments are regarded seriously important, especially when they happen to be the pleading petitions of the Son of God to his heavenly Father. "I pray," he implored, "that they all may be one"; "I pray that" this motley crew of people, summoned and recruited from all walks of life, "not many wise, not many mighty, not many noble" (1 Corinthians 1:26), whose only commonality, connecting one life with the other, was their faith in Christ and Christ's faith in them, "may be one."

After all, in a few short hours he would be crucified. The only legacy he could leave was a company of people, unimpressive, unpromising, some dredged up from the lowest levels of human society, whose common affliction was poverty and whose uniform liability was powerlessness. And he was aware of his calling as Savior of the world and Redeemer of the cosmos, and that he possessed incredibly unpromising collaborators who easily lost nerve; and he knew that before many hours would pass, the most articulate of his disciples and most daring of his followers would stoop to the cowardice of denial and conceal any admission of identity and hide from the perils of loyalty.

What was there for the Lord to do? He prayed! The future of the world was being shaped by that prayer. How strange that the One possessed of omnipotence to whom "all authority in heaven and earth" was to be given, with all the power to refashion and reshape the world, prayed, "Father," "Holy Father," "O Righteous Father." And what did he pray to the Father? "[I pray] that they all may be one; even as thou, Father, art in me, and I in thee, that they also may be in us, so that the world may believe that thou hast sent me" (John 17:22). Why did he pray at that crucial moment "that they all may be one"? Why is the unity of the church so crucial?

I

Could it be that the Lord himself had enormous needs in this hour; the need of fellowship, the need of love, the need of a supportive community, who would share in his sufferings and agonies and assure him of their devotion and loyalty? "Even as thou, Father, art in me, and I in thee," so he longed and ached for the intimacy with his people, with his church: "that they also may be in us." And the intimacy he longed for between himself and his people, he prayed would be true between his people also, a unity and fusion, as profound and meaningful and spiritual as the union between husband and wife. "Therefore a man leaves his father and his mother and cleaves to his wife, and they become one flesh" (Genesis 2:24).

Crisis lays bare what really counts and endures in life—strips away the superfluous, removes the accessories, peels away the supplementary, and removes the nonessential—until what remains is the irreducible heart of reality. Our Lord, who himself is never shielded with the superfluous, nevertheless, as his supreme moment of crisis approached, found himself falling back to the bedrock of his reassurance, the ultimate ground of his being, his intimacy with his Father: "Thou, Father, art in me, and I in thee." But what is so arresting is his impulse of longing for intimacy with his people: "that they also may be in us."

It is one of the sad indexes of our time that the word "intimacy" evokes primarily images of sexuality so that an intimate relationship is perceived basically in sexual terms. Perhaps this is a clue toward judgment and hope. It could be a judgment of the rarity and uncommonness of relationships of depth and profound familiarity between people today; our very language betrays our poverty, the erosion of meaning, and the stilted, limited range familiarity carries today. Language, like art, is a reliable indicator of the human condition. But the imagery of sex in relation to intimacy may also provide clues in our search for meaning. There is no human relationship that expresses such depth of love and the union of two personalities and the fusion of wills and the intermingling of hearts and minds as the union between husband and wife: "For this reason a man shall leave his father and mother and be joined to his wife and the two shall become one flesh," writes Paul (Ephesians 5:31). "This is a great mystery: but I speak concerning Christ and the church," (Ephesians 5:32, KJV). Union between husband and wife is a parable, illustrating, pictorializing, imaging for our understanding God's will and purpose, of the range and depth and quality in interpersonal relationship expected and anticipated.

Therefore, when Christ prayed that "they all may be one," he was praying that the relationship prevailing in the church be as profoundly intimate and sacred and self-giving as the mystery of marriage between man and woman. What a daring imagery! Yet it's there in the Bible, freely used by Paul and other biblical writers, which indicates the sacredness of sexual relationship in the sight of God, so far removed from its common association with lust and lasciviousness.

Could it be that our current obsession with sex and the demand for sexual freedom are cultural indicators of the erosion of intimacy and the absence of deep levels of loving community in the home, in the church, in the world, and the desperate compensatory grasp for the touch and experience of intimacy through the only channel one thinks available? The hunger for sexuality may in fact ultimately arise out of the longing for fellowship, for love, to be in touch with the profoundest levels of reality, hidden in the mysterious untouchable depths. It may be the instinct to probe the hiddenness of life, to plumb the depths, the heights, and breadth of life because life is frustration and unfulfilled torment when we are shut out of its secret chambers of mystery.

Paul is not loathe to use the most intimate imagery to express the relationship between Christ and his church: "Husbands, love your wives, as Christ loved the church and gave himself up for her" (Ephesians 5:25); "Even so husbands should love their wives as their own bodies. He who loves his wife loves himself. For no man ever hates his own flesh, but nourishes and cherishes it, as Christ does the church, because we are members of his body" (Ephesians 5:29-30). Contemporary nuns, when they take their vows of celibacy, poverty, and obedience, in a real sense take vows of wedlock, to be wedded permanently and eternally to their Lord, even wearing a ring as sign of that marriage, which in a sense is symbolization of the relationship between Christ and the church. We are the Bride of Christ.

Therefore, the prayer of our Lord was a prayer that in the face of history's most testing crisis the central nature and hope of the universe be preserved and not destroyed; this threat of destruction was a threat to this core of reality, namely, the intimacy between Father and Son and between Christ and his people and between the people themselves. Therefore the unity he prays for is the unity in the Godhead gathering up the unity of the world into the unity of the Godhead, so that "we are to grow up in every way into him who is the head, into Christ" (Ephesians 4:15) so that "Christ is all, and in all" (Colossians 3:11). We have scaled mountains, plumbed oceans, traversed the plains, and mined the wealth of the earth. We have even conquered space and reached the moon. What we must now do is explore the mystery of God and search the mystery of humankind, those worlds more awesome and vast than the world of space and planets. We must probe the inner dimensions of God, penetrate inside of God to find our way into God; we must probe the inner mysteries to know what it means to be one with him, internalized by him, embraced and loved by him. To love God and to glorify him forever is, after all, the end and purpose of life.

The other side of the coin is to learn and explore the deep mysteries of human personality to learn how to get inside the life of another, for after these centuries, we are least knowledgeable of each other; we are inscrutable worlds coexisting, strangers to each other, denying and depriving each other of our inner worlds, keeping these precious and priceless possessions even from those who are closest to us. Because we live in a world where we have not the intimacy of unity, we have largely kept ourselves under the lock and key of our protected solitude and privacy. Concerning a former member of a local church, I heard it said that very few knew him well. Isn't this true with most of us? Aren't we cautious and reluctant to trust each other to the degree that we establish a deep relationship, since we expect our relationships to be fleeting and transient and ephemeral? How many of your current friendships do you anticipate to endure into the future, even after you move away to another community? With some of you, your closest relationships are not with people in your church but elsewhere. But our Lord prayed "that they all may be one even as we are one," which means that all members are to be wedded and joined together in a relationship of intimacy, a relationship which brings joy and delight to be together, and pain and loneliness to be apart. I believe you must all decide where your ultimate sense of community and fellowship and social familyhood should lodge. You must have that place of trust and reliance, your linkage into God's vast world of promise and kingdom, and it should be your local church. That is what the local congregation is meant to be in the plan and purpose of God. You cannot survive as human beings made in the image of God without being intimately wedded into a loving community of mutual support and reciprocal esteem.

So the unity of the church we pray for is not simply unity between the denominations or between Rome and Geneva, or between the evangelicals and the liberals, or an ecumenism which embraces all churches inside and outside the National and the World Council of Churches. It is at least that, but it means more than that.

II

"So that the world may believe that thou hast sent me" (John 17:21). What seems apparent is that the world acknowledging Christ as Lord, therefore under obligation and accountability to him, will be determined largely by the church's life of unity and intimacy. On Easter Sunday we point out that the resurrection was the event of public declaration of Christ's lordship over the world, that the world had entered into a new order, with Christ as the promise of its ultimate transformation into the kingdom of God. Therefore in this time of God's history, it is the response of the nations, the response of the world to the lordship of Jesus Christ which is the center of God's purpose, "that the world may believe that thou hast sent me." It's the relationship of the whole world to Christ which is the purpose of the gospel, not just a part of the world represented in the church. This implies that the world can acknowledge Christ as Lord without becoming a part of the church, but the church is that small community in the world whose unity will evoke and enable the world to acknowledge Christ as their Lord.

This means that the church's role is at least twofold: that we become a community of intimacy and unity with Christ and each other, and that we proclaim with a sense of finality the lordship of

Jesus Christ over the world. There is nothing that impresses the world more than an authentic, profound experience of God; and so insistent is its demand for authenticity that the world is critically sensitive of any marks and signs of inauthenticity, anything which borders on fraudulence. And there is nothing which earns the world's scorn and contempt more than a religious fraud, because the world possesses an instinctive abhorrence of exploiting the holy, so that sacrilege is more contemptible than almost any human sin. The soul of the world, I believe, longs to see authentic piety, genuine and profound knowledge of God, the awful sense of awe before the almighty God, true holy men and women. When they see genuine piety, they take hope. They take hope in the sense that someone is in a representative capacity on their behalf, believing in God and worshiping him; and in that representative act they find meaning. It is vicarious participation by the world, like the Memphis garbage collectors who vicariously took pride in Martin Luther King, and the youth in Harlem who vicariously appropriate and claim for themselves the achievement of their black athletic stars. The world takes heart when it sees the church portray genuine piety in its knowledge and awe of God, for the church's faith on the world's behalf as a representative community becomes the vicarious faith of the world. Then the world acknowledges the lordship of Christ through the faith of the church. Remember Paul and Silas saying to the Roman jailer: "Believe in the Lord Jesus, and you will be saved, you and your household" (Acts 16:31). The faith of the church affects the whole human household, which is the meaning of ecumenism, coming from the Greek word "oikumene."

The world is also eager to see evidence of genuine community, visible signs of true unity and intimacy, actually being lived out. The outward brusqueness and seeming indifference to any loving fellowship simply conceal a hunger to find such possibilities. Isn't it because the human heart seeks for such and does not find it that so many seek therapy from psychiatrists and counselors? That is the prevailing practice in a city like New York. And for a brief period, at a high price, lonely souls seek the magic of human relationship and human dialogue, communication and discourse; and group therapies provide simulated experiences of fellowship and intimacy.

The whole world is crying out, in muffled tones to be sure, for any signs anywhere in the world, of the actual existence of a creatively intimate community of people, who have broken down the barriers of silence and live in open dialogue and trustful intimacy with each other. Even the editor of *Saturday Review* writes with mingled nostalgia and hope about the Amish communities of Pennsylvania. Why have your sons and daughters in the 1960s formed and joined communes? And certainly, many of you have vicariously taken pride in the Koinonia Farm of Americus, Georgia, founded by Clarence Jordan. What is the secret power that attracts middle-class young people to the strange and questionable Moon movement and the Unification Church? What is the central genius of every Christian movement among the young, whether Campus Crusade, Youth for Christ, Young Life, Inter-Varsity Christian Fellowship, and others? It's the sense of belonging to a community, bound together by ties of a common faith and love for each other; it's a commitment to Christ and a commitment to one another. How desperately young people need that! How desperately we all need that! In fact, that is the meaning of salvation, to be saved and rescued out of our isolation and aloneness into the joys of a warm and powerful relationship of intimacy and love with Christ and with a community of people. Hell is the sense of being left alone. Heaven is the reality of being included and embraced and wanted and loved by God and a community of people.

Appendix:
A Case Study

Emmanuel Baptist Church in Ridgewood, New Jersey, is a suburban church of medium size, still considered one of the leading American Baptist churches of the state, but considerably reduced in membership from its days of the revival of church attendance of the fifties and sixties. But the church is made up of people of unusual quality, of middle-class affluence, who take their faith and loyalty to the church very seriously and take legitimate pride in their history. But the most serious question facing them is their future. Is the decline in membership of the past decade an indicator of their future? While numerical and statistical data do not provide ultimate significance, can there be meaning for a congregation even in the face of a declining attendance? Why cannot Emmanuel, situated in a substantial community like Ridgewood, grow numerically?

Thus the issue of church growth is very much in the center of thinking of the people of Emmanuel. We assumed this to be a legitimate concern, not to be repudiated as simply arising out of concerns for institutional survival. So, Church Growth was proposed to the Boards of Deacons and Christian Education to become the theme for study during the period of Lent (1978) for the whole congregation. Eight Lenten Bible Study classes (seven adult and one youth) were scheduled, six on Sunday mornings, one on Sunday nights, one on Wednesday mornings. Eight teachers, with an equal number of backup people, were recruited; most of them were theologically trained ministers who are also members of the congregation. Their thorough preparation for their classes began weeks in advance of Lent. Exhibit A contains the introductory material for those studies.

Despite the common practice of people attending morning worship but not church school to pursue Bible study, the registration and attendance in these eight classes was most encouraging. A Study Guide was developed, mainly through the initiative and work of Dr. Donald Wheeler, one of the teachers; and the Guide is included very much as it was circulated through the Emmanuel Congregation. I began the series in my Sunday morning sermons a few weeks in advance, beginning with "Why Bible Study?" and a general introduction on "Can the Church Grow?" Then I dealt with the Bible study themes in each Sunday morning sermon beginning with "Unfinished Creation." The printed sermon of the previous Sunday became available as one of the study resources for the following Bible study classes. Thus a dialogical relationship was established between the pulpit and the pew, and an obvious sense of anticipation unfolded as each subject related to Church Growth.

Two weeks after the completion of the Lenten Series, an all-day Church Planning Retreat took place; members at this retreat reflected on the Bible Study on Church Growth and attempted to see their implication on the plan and program for the church for the coming year. It reflected the mood of the congregation that an interim period was not time simply to wait for the coming of the new minister, and to hold everything in abeyance, but a time for planning and action, so that the new minister would need to "jump on a moving train." The retreat identified seven major goals, closely related to the seven themes on Church Growth; reflected on provisional objectives and tactics; and agreed to recommend them for church adoption.

These goals were adopted by the church, and each board is currently in the process of determining specific strategies on how they might achieve these goals during the coming year. The seven goals and some provisional strategies are included in this case study report. Exhibit B contains the material developed in that retreat.

EXHIBIT A

Bible Study on Church Growth

"GROW UP IN EVERY WAY INTO CHRIST"

A Lenten Bible Study Guide

on

Church Growth

February 12—March 26, 1978

Eight Study Groups

Sundays 9:30 A.M.; Sundays 7:00 P.M.; Wednesdays 10:30 A.M.

EMMANUEL BAPTIST CHURCH
14 Hope Street
Ridgewood, New Jersey

Invitation to Growth

The great Christian thinker, Emil Brunner once said, "The church exists by mission, just as fire exists by burning."[1] Without mission the church is dead. Church growth is a product of mission.

During Lent, 1978, we will do something unprecedented for Emmanuel Baptist Church (correct me if you know better). We will focus the attention of the whole congregation on the question of church growth through our worship, Bible study, and personal religious life; all of this will culminate in an All Church Planning Retreat.

The time is right for such concentrated effort. First of all, our church must convey the Christian faith more vigorously and effectively to the coming generation in our community and beyond. We need more hands and hearts given over to this task. Secondly, we have the talented leadership of Dr. Jitsuo Morikawa, who has given himself for a lifetime to the task of taking the whole gospel to the whole world. He has stimulated our thinking and inspired this effort.

However, nothing is possible without the dedicated participation of Emmanuel people. Join in as many ways as you can.

Sunday Morning Worship

Let us give prayerful consideration to church growth. Dr. Morikawa will preach on the Bible study theme to be taken up the subsequent Sunday in the Bible study groups. We will receive the sermon with *expectations*.

Lenten Bible Studies on Church Growth

Eight groups led by members of the church will search the Scriptures to understand God's purposes regarding church growth.

Home Worship and Study

We can consider God's purposes for church growth through using the Scripture selections in this study guide and Dr. Morikawa's sermons. We encourage everyone to read the Acts of the Apostles, Ephesians, and Colossians before Easter.

All Church Planning Retreat on Church Growth

On April 8, the church family will join together to set program priorities for the coming year. Recommendations will be forwarded to the church boards for action.

Church Council and Boards

The responsible church boards will consider and act on proposals. Board members should be part of the whole process of study.

One Final Word

It is of the utmost importance that our study and fellowship result in new priorities and programs, We should evaluate *our emphasis* on church growth by the *"fruit" it bears* for church growth.

William and Mildred Patrick
Donald and Judy Wheeler
Stanley and Helen Stuber
Frank and Virginia Leeds
Peg and Donald Sherman
Nancy Shaver and Bob Elfers
William Holderith and
    Dan Busdiecker
Miriam Eckard, Leonard and
    Nancy Ballesteros

BIBLE STUDY LEADERS

"GROW UP IN EVERY WAY INTO CHRIST"

A Lenten Bible Study Guide

on

Church Growth

Preface

Bible study on church growth does not sound earthshaking to say the least. It is deceptively unobtrusive, disarmingly unexciting, and unpretentious in its apparent claim. But like the power of life, through its tenacious roots and fibers, silently and invisibly penetrating even the wall of resistant rock, until boulders are known to be split by the mystery of silent power, so the event of the simple act of Bible study around the theme of church growth may turn out excitingly significant!

The unpretentious theme does have the ability to evoke pursuit through winding labyrinthian caverns and channels of surprising mystery exposing us to new worlds of meaning heretofore unknown to many of us. In fact it can, like so many famous restaurants housed in unpretentious, uninviting quarters, serve as a simple gateway into a rich world. Church growth as a theme has the unusual evocative capacity of surfacing some of the major global and theological issues of our times and certainly can deal with the central affirmations of the gospel.

Church growth is a subsidiary activity. The primary movement is the growth of the cosmos to maturity and consummation, "to grow up in every way into him who is the head, into Christ" (Ephesians 4:15). Church growth is a sign in history of the growth of the universe; by living that future in the present, the church is a witness to this future hope of the cosmos.

1. The Church as a Sign and Firstfruit of the Consummation: Unfinished Creation

That the universe in which we live is an unfinished universe in the process of development and growth is supported both by science and the Bible. The billions of years of our planet's history, discerned by science, and the biblical story of God's encounter and relationship to the human family testify to his amazing, patient, long-suffering shaping and reshaping of his universe; these two facts testify to the unfinished character of the universe and thus God summoning his people into partnership to complete his work of creation and redemption. This means that God takes this world with utmost seriousness; it is a world he created, to which he sent his Son, and in the midst of which he is ever present. The renewal and completion of this world, of this planet, of this universe, is his ultimate purpose. Therefore, the question to be considered in light of the suggested biblical material is: *What* is the relation between church growth and the unfinished character of the universe?

Romans 8:19-23

Ephesians 2 (especially vv. 10, 14-22)

Genesis 3-4; 11:1-9

Exodus 34 (especially vv. 6-10, 17-35)

John 1

2. God's Kingdom on Earth: The Ultimate End of Growth

There is something larger than the church, of which the church is only part, in fact, for which the church is the means. Therefore, the growth of the church is not in itself its ultimate end and purpose, but the purpose of the church is to aid the growth of the cosmos, the development of the universe, to completion and consummation, to the full realization of the kingdom of God. We call this eschatology.

> Eschatology means the doctrine of the Christian hope, which embraces both the object hoped for and also the hope inspired by it. From first to last, and not merely in the epilogue, Christianity is eschatology, is hope, forward looking and forward moving, and therefore also revolutionizing and transforming the present.[1]

Therefore, the question is, what is the relationship between church growth and growth of the cosmos to completion? The following references speak to this relationship.

Genesis 1-2
Ephesians 1 (especially 1:9-10)
Colossians 1 (especially vv. 15-20)
Philippians 2:5-11 (especially vv. 10-11)
Matthew 6:9-10
Luke 17:21
Revelation 21 (especially vv. 1-4, 22-27)

3. All Together in One Place: Numerical Growth

It must be made clear that the Bible in no way assumes that the growth of the church numerically is finished until the whole world and the whole human family are in the church. There are evidences of numerical growth in the Bible, as in the book of Acts; however, the purpose of the church is not to displace the world or win the world into its life and being. But rather, the church is always a small part of the world, called by God to be in the world, as a redemptive force, like salt and leaven, that the whole lump of the world be leavened and the whole of humanity be preserved and redeemed. While the church may be a minority, God's love and concern, embracing without exception "the all," are for the whole world, every nation, all humanity. The expansion of the church is a means to the growth of righteousness, the expansion of justice:

> Let justice roll down like water,
>   and righteousness like an everflowing stream.
> —Amos 5:24

Therefore, the question is: If numerical growth of the church is not its end goal, then what is the purpose and value of numerical growth?

Acts (especially 2:1-13, 44ff.; 4:4; 11:20-26)
   When there is growth, whose work is it, and under what conditions does it occur?
Revelation 7:9
   Can you sense any connection between the numbers and the inclusiveness of the group? Compare with Acts 2:1-13.
Genesis 12:1-3; 13:14-17
   One Abraham, many descendants.

4. Power to Comprehend the Love of Christ: Reflective Growth

Reflecting on the insights laid out in the Scriptures, we must know who we are as designed and purposed by God. How essential our Lord took this to be is reflected in the frequency with which he "taught" his disciples; and the teaching curriculum of the Bible is massive, called "didache" in contrast to "kerygma" or proclamation. The Letters of Paul appeal to the *mind* as well as the heart, that we "may have power to comprehend with all the saints what is the breadth and length and height and depth" (Ephesians 3:18). We are all called to be "lay theologians," that we may be given a "spirit of wisdom and of revelation in the knowledge of him, having the eyes of your hearts enlightened" (Ephesians 1:17-18), to avoid "misunderstanding of the church"[2] and falling prey to the subtle heresies which are constantly afflicting the church. Therefore, the question is: How seriously are we taking Bible study and theological reflection in our church? Consider the following Scripture references:

> Ephesians 1:18
> > 3:14-19
> > 4:11-32 (especially 11-24)
> Matthew 28:18-19
> Acts 2:42
> Romans 12:1-2 (especially 2, ". . . by the renewal of your mind. . . .")

5. Building Up the Body of Christ: Organic Growth

The biblical images of growth are surprisingly scant in terms of individual growth, but numerous in terms of corporate growth, the growth of Israel as a people of God, and the growth of the church as the body of Christ. And the ethics of the Bible, whether love, humility, gentleness, or meekness, are all social ethics, behavioral patterns in relation to neighbor, rarely private ethics unrelated to other human beings. This of course is based on the assumption that we cannot be authentic persons except in the context of community, and the development of living models of community life is the persistent need of our civilization. Therefore, the question is: What does it mean to grow organically as a body of Christ? Does this require as much serious consideration on our part as does personal growth? Consider the following passages.

> Romans 12
> 1 Corinthians 12-13
> Philippians 2:1-11
> 1 Peter 2:1-10

6. Thy Kingdom Come on Earth: Growth in Transformative Impact

"What is the Church for?" was the question Hendrick

Kraemer kept asking. Is it to recruit more people into the church? Is the purpose of an army to recruit more soldiers, who in turn will recruit more soldiers? For what purpose are soldiers finally recruited? What is the church for? The church is a means, an instrument, a servant community to serve the world, to bear witness to the world thus creating a crisis of decision, "the power of judgment in the sense of discernment, the ability to distinguish what is for his good and what is for his ill." Thus "a ferment had been let loose in history that 'turned the world upside down' wherever it spread."[3] Therefore, the question is: What is the difference between the conversion of the church and the transformation of the world? Consider these biblical sources:

Matthew 5:13-14; 13:31-33
2 Corinthians 5:11-20
Matthew 25
Luke 4:16-21; 7:22
Hebrews 13:8-16 (especially vv. 12-14)
Isaiah 52–53
Jonah (especially 4:9-11)
Acts 17:6
Micah 6:6-8
Amos 5:21-24
Luke 10:25-37
Luke 6; Matthew 5-7

7. The Body of Christ: Growth in Unity

We saw that the unity and reconciliation of the whole universe in Christ is the ultimate and final end of God's purpose. But the eschatological reality declares that the consummating event to occur in the "final age" of God's history, the "Last Days," the "End Times," have already begun, for we are already in the climactic "end times" of God's great purpose. And one of the signs of the "Last Days" is the presence of the church, as a vivid and living sign of this final age, the age of culmination. And the crucial mark of the church as a sign of the imminent unity of the world in Christ is its own unity, the unity of the church. Therefore, the great priestly prayer of our Lord on which the Ecumenical Movement hinges is: "I do not pray for these only, but also for those who believe in me through their word, that they all may be one; even as thou, Father, art in me, and I in thee, that they also may be in us, so that the world may believe that thou hast sent me" (John 17:20-21). Therefore, the question is: What is the relationship between the unity of the church and evangelism in the world? How do the following Scripture references speak to this question?

Isaiah 2:1-4
Revelation 21
John 17
1 Corinthians 15

EXHIBIT B
Church Planning Retreat

Following the Church Planning Retreat chaired by Don and Peg Sherman, the retreat planning committee mailed to the whole congregation the results and recommendations of the planning retreat in terms of preliminary goals. At the following meeting of the official boards, these goals and strategies were discussed and examined in several groups using the following worksheet which summarized the recommendations. Although the goals were officially adopted, a continuing refining process is anticipated for which a further planning retreat is scheduled. The following worksheet simply indicates a step in the total process of study and reflection issuing in planning for program and action in a local church. This document is presented without substantive or editorial change, but as a raw sample of planning in one local congregation, exactly in the form it appeared in the haste and excitement of an actual community of busy lay people, written by them, reflecting their energy and vision and dedication to the life of the Spirit.

Work Sheet for Selection
of 1978–1979 Objectives/Strategies
to Achieve Seven Major Goals
Emmanuel Baptist Church
Ridgewood, New Jersey

A Summary of Directions and Priorities from the Retreat
of April 8, 1978, Stony Point, New York

INSTRUCTIONS: The following purpose, 7 goals and 33 specific objectives/strategies to achieve them, are the edited results of the recommendations of the discussion groups which met during the Church Retreat on April 8, 1978. The 7 goals are the challenge presented to Retreat participants by Dr. Morikawa. Now they must be considered, modified and finally adopted by Emmanuel's "Official Family"—the Council and Combined Boards. The task of each of the discussion groups is to review the assigned goal and objectives and report back the following to the plenary session of the Combined Boards:
  1. Objectives recommended for approval
  2. Objectives revised for approval

3. Additional objectives recommended for approval
4. Board(s) or Council responsible for developing action programs to achieve the objectives

PRIMARY PURPOSE—The purpose of the Emmanuel Baptist Church is to heed the admonition of St. Paul to "grow up in every way into him who is the head, into Christ." (Ephesians 4:15)

Goal 1. The gospel is ultimate hope in action. Therefore, we intend to live the present in the light of the ultimate purpose of God.

Objectives

(A) Train ourselves to live the future in the present

(B) Evaluate in depth the Christian Education program in terms of its effectiveness for living in the present and the future

(C) Reassess our church property to determine changes required to serve most effectively and efficiently the present and future needs of the church program

(D) Be supportive of the new minister

(E)

(F)

Goal 2. We live in an unfinished, developing universe. Therefore, we will seek to live in anticipation of newness.

Approved	Council	Decisions	Educ.	Missions	Trustees

Objectives:

(A) Experiment with new forms of worship, using youth and adult laity

(B) Seek a unique ministry to characterize Emmanuel's mission in Bergen County—elderly—race track ministry

(C) Explore and test new ideas

(D)

(E)

Goal 3. We are called to love God with all our heart, strength and mind. Therefore, we will engage in rigorous, organized reflection.

Objectives:

(A) Continue educational opportunities, with focus on preparation for achieving church goals

(B) Plan two spiritual retreats during the year

(C) Emphasize stewardship education

(D) Develop strong program for youth and young adults

(E) Encourage entire congregation to participate in Bible Study

(F) Seek more participation in training conference opportunities

(G)

Approved	Council	Decisions	Educ.	Missions	Trustees

Goal 4. The Kingdom of God is to be a fellowship of all people, nations and races. Therefore, we will reach out to become an inclusive fellowship of believers

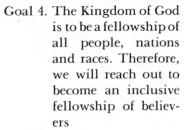

Objectives:
- (A) Invite more young couples to join our fellowship
- (B) Seek racial, economic and theological diversity
- (C) Reach out to senior high youth and young adults
- (D) Organize an Evangelism Committee
- (E) Continue and improve ways to reach potential members (Church visitor staff position)
- (F)
- (G)

Goal 5. The gospel is corporate as well as personal. Therefore, we will strive to achieve organizational effectiveness as the Body of Christ.

Objectives:
- (A) Communicate church family concerns more effectively
- (B) Establish strong endowment program
- (C) Develop plan for achieving more effective utilization of

members' talents

(D) Improve communication of in-church policy decisions and programs

(E) Conduct annual planning and calendar-building retreat for church members

(F) Implement and coordinate systematic long-range planning and performance evaluation, related to program and budget building

(G) Appoint Ombudsman to handle any concern of any member

(H) Appoint pastor's liaison committee to appraise, counsel and support minister

(I)

(J)

Goal 6. Christ came to minister to the world and called us to His ministry. Therefore, we will work to equip the laity for ministry in the world.

Objectives:

(A) Increase youth and adult participation in ecumenical, denominational and Bergen County projects

(B) Reach out with ourselves and our money to serve those with special needs: (prisons, tutoring, aging, hunger, etc.)

(C) Identify and provide opportunities for sharing individual members' service in the world

(D) Present our church opportunities to the public

(E)

(F)

Goal 7. We are all members of the Body of Christ and members one of another. Therefore, we intend to become an intimate and concerned community of believers.

Objectives:

(A) Develop a sense of being a church family (all church gatherings, etc.)

(B) Experiment with the extended family concept

(C) Expand small group fellowship through monthly special interest groups involving every member of the church

(D)

Approved	Council	Decisions	Educ.	Missions	Trustees

Notes

Chapter 1: Why Bible Study?

[1] John B. Cobb, Jr., "Can the Church Think Again?" in the United Methodist Church of Higher Education and Ministry: Occasional Paper, vol. 1, no. 12 (August 9, 1976), p. 3.

[2] George Steiner, "The Lollipopping of the West," *New York Times*, December 9, 1977, p. 27.

Chapter 2: Are We Growing?

[1] James Reston, "Carter and the Congress," *New York Times*, January 18, 1978, p. A21.

Chapter 3: Unfinished Creation

[1] Jo Thomas, "U.S. Sues to Recover Pension Fund Losses in Teamsters' Plan," *New York Times*, February 2, 1978, p. A1.

[2] Eric Rust, "The Incarnation and Ecology: A Theological Perspective," p. 3. (An unpublished manuscript, used as the basis for an address presented by Dr. Rust at a conference on church growth sponsored by American Baptist National Ministries in September, 1977.)

[3] *Ibid.*, p. 6.

[4] *Ibid.*, p. 4.

[5] Dietrich Bonhoeffer, *Ethics*, ed. Eberhard Bethge (New York: Macmillan, Inc., 1955), p. 65.

[6] *Ibid.*

[7] Herbert Marcuse, *One-Dimensional Man* (Boston: Beacon Press, 1964).

[8] George Adam Smith, "Atheism of Force and Atheism of Fear," in *The Book of Isaiah*, vol. 1 (New York: Doubleday & Company, Inc., 1927), pp. 171-182.

[9] Paul Tillich, *The New Being* (New York: Charles Scribner's Sons, 1955).

[10] Henri J. M. Nouwen and Walter J. Gaffney, *Aging* (Garden City, N.Y.: Doubleday & Company, Inc., 1974), pp. 17-45.

[11] *Ibid.*, pp. 47-81.

[12] *Ibid.*, p. 51.

[13] *Ibid.*, p. 56.

Chapter 4: The Ultimate End of Church Growth

[1] Leonard Silk, "Boulding's Interests Range from Trivial to the Cosmic," *New York Times*, December 30, 1977, p. D1.

[2] Edward Fiske, "It's a Different Yale, as a New Blue Takes Over," *New York Times*, December 25, 1977, Section 4, p. 7.

[3] B. Drummond Ayres, Jr., "Henry Ford, at Conference, Leads Critics of Federal Business Rules," *New York Times*, January 31, 1978, p. 24.

[4] Jürgen Moltmann, *Theology of Hope* (New York: Harper & Row, Publishers, 1967), p. 16.

[5] Hans J. Margull, *Hope in Action* (Philadelphia: Muhlenberg Press, 1962, incorporated into Fortress Press), p. xix.

Chapter 5: Numerical Growth of the Church

[1] Pitirim A. Sorokin, *The Crisis of Our Age: The Social and Cultural Outlook* (New York: E. P. Dutton & Co., Inc., 1943), p. 252.

[2] *Ibid.*, p. 255.

[3] Hendrik Kraemer, *A Theology of the Laity* (Philadelphia: The Westminster Press, 1958) p. 127.

[4] Hans-Ruedi Weber, "God's Arithmetic," p. 13; a shorter version of a document published in *Frontier*, IV, vol. 6 (Winter, 1963), London.

[5] Kazoh Kitamori, *Theology of the Pain of God* (Richmond, Va.: John Knox Press, 1965), p. 19.

[6] Sören Kierkegaard, *Philosophical Fragments*, trans. David F. Swenson (Princeton: Princeton University Press, 1962), pp. xx-xxi.

[7] Steven Rattner, "West Virginia and Indiana Order Power Reduction in Coal Strike," *New York Times*, February 14, 1978. p. 1.

[8] Frank Greve, "Ugly Truth: Society Prefers Pretty People," *Philadelphia Inquirer*, February 13, 1978, p. 4-A.

Chapter 6: Reflective Growth of the Church

[1] James Reston, "The Hidden News," *New York Times*, February 22, 1978, p. A23.

[2] Edward B. Fiske, "Ethics Courses Now Attracting Many More U.S. College Students,"*New York Times*, February 20, 1978, p. A1.

[3] Robert N. Bellah, *The Broken Covenant: American Civil Religion in Time of Trial* (New York: The Seabury Press, Inc., 1976), p. 1.

[4] John Kenneth Galbraith, *The Affluent Society* (New York: New American Library, 1970), p. 22; Alexander Miller, *The Christian Significance of Karl Marx* (New York: Macmillan, Inc., n.d.), p. 15.

[5] John B. Cobb, Jr., "Can the Church Think Again?" in the United Methodist Church of Higher Education and Ministry: Occasional Paper, vol. 1, no. 12 (August 9, 1976), p. 1.

[6] Galbraith, *op. cit.*, frontispiece.

[7] Reston, *op. cit.*

Chapter 7: Organic Growth of the Church

[1] Robert N. Bellah, *The Broken Covenant* (New York: The Seabury Press, Inc., 1976), p. 1.

[2] Hendrik Kraemer, *The Communication of the Christian Faith* (Philadelphia: The Westminster Press, 1956), p. 20.

[3] H. Richard Niebuhr, *The Purpose of the Church and Its Ministry* (New York: Harper & Row, Publishers, 1977), p. 31.

Chapter 8: Growth in Transformative Impact

[1] Johannes Blauw, *The Missionary Nature of the Church* (New York: McGraw-Hill Book Company, Inc., 1962), p. 83.

[2] See *ibid.*

[3] Henry W. Clark, *The Cross and the Eternal Order* (New York: Macmillan, Inc., 1944).

[4] John S. Dunne, *Time and Myth* (Garden City: Doubleday & Company, 1973), p. 6.

[5] Oscar Cullmann, *Christ and Time: The Primitive Christian Conception of Time and History*, trans. Floyd V. Filson (Philadelphia: The Westminster Press, 1964), p. 179.

[6] Elizabeth O'Connor, *Journey Inward, Journey Outward* (New York: Harper & Row, Publishers, 1968), p. 36.

[7] David Tracy, *Blessed Rage for Order: The New Pluralism in Theology* (New York: A Crossroad Book, imprint of The Seabury Press, Inc., 1975), p. 8.

[8] Arnold B. Come, *Agents of Reconciliation* (Philadelphia: The Westminster Press, 1960), pp. 150-151.

Bible Study on Church Growth

[1] Jürgen Moltmann, *Theology of Hope* (New York: Harper & Row, Publishers, 1967), p. 16.

[2] Emil Brunner, *The Misunderstanding of the Church* (Philadelphia: The Westminster Press, 1953).

[3] Arnold B. Come, *Agents of Reconciliation* (Philadelphia: The Westminster Press, 1960), p. 155.

Appendix, Exhibit A

[1] Emil Brunner, *The Word and the World* (Lexington, Ky.: Keystone Printery, 1965, reprint, American Theological Library Association), p. 108.